A NEW HOME

YOUR NEED TO FIT IN IS PREVENTING YOU
FROM STANDING OUT.

BRYAN PHARR

A NEW HOME by Bryan Pharr

Published by IEXIST Publishing

This book or parts thereof may not be reproduced in any form, stored in a retrieval system or transmitted in any form by any means – electronic, mechanical, photocopy, recording or otherwise – without prior written permission of the publisher, except as provided by United Stated of America copyright law.

Copyright © 2018 by Bryan Pharr
All rights reserved

ISBN 978-0692099681

To my wife Deitra – thank you for walking this journey with me!

- Love, Bryan

"…But for the overlooked, the outcast, the rejected, the misfit that dared for more, the truth was always there - the truth of "A NEW HOME", the truth of a better home…a home for us all."

- "A New Home" - Chapter I
(Written by Bryan Pharr)

I. THE LIFE OF A BLACK SHEEP
I. MISTAKE
II. BUS PASSES AND FASHION SENSE
III. TEMPORARY BLINDNESS
IV. DREAMWEAVER
V. DARK FANTASIES
VI. LOST

II. TRANSIT
VII. WAVE RUNNER
VIII. BACK TO BACK
IX. GOD CONTRADICTION
X. REBEL
XI. JOURNEY
XII. CLARITY

III. A NEW HOME
XIII. WHERE TO?
XIV. A KING AND A PAUPER
XV. ALONE
XVI. DIFFERENT
XVII. ICON
XVIII. LEGACY

A NEW HOME

Chapter I:

Foxes have holes and birds have nests but the Son-of-Man has nowhere to lay his head...

- The Christ

The Life of a Black Sheep

A Dead Giveaway
(Introduction)

After thinking many hours (seemingly) over how I would start this story, under the immense pressure of writing my first work to be published, I've decided to go all out. I'm going to do what no self-respecting author would do. I'm going to do what no master of storytelling would do. Here it is: I'm going to tell you EXACTLY what this book is about! As a matter of fact, if you were savvy enough to read into the chapter heading (I'm certain you are), you already know. This entire book is about finding your place. I apologize if you're the type that won't go see a movie if someone even gives you the slightest peek into its storyline. I too am this type of person. But don't worry your heart. Although I've clued you in, I'm more than confident that you'll find something written within these pages that you can relate to and that will help you better navigate your life. I won't promise that this book will cover all of the complexities of the issue. I can already tell that as life goes on, a few revisions may be in order. But I will assure you that you won't regret the read.

My life's story thus far, like many of yours, has been filled with a multitude of ups and downs. What I have now realized is that a great deal of them have all revolved, in retrospect, around a singular issue. That is the issue of identity. Not knowing where you "fit in" in life can present a unique set of struggles that if we aren't carful, can send any one of us into some dark places internally and will eventually, always reflect in external issues. Bending and boxing ourselves, or just completely throwing our true natures by the wayside

A New Home

in order to replace what we should be for what we could be, are just a few examples of the pressures life can present when we are void of our true identities. So many of us have chosen that way of living and because of it, continually go through cycles of being unsure, unsuccessful and unfulfilled. At the core, it is identity that is often linked to all of these adverse effects experienced throughout our individual journeys.

I wrote this book from my experience. I wrote it for myself, for those of you who I've come in contact with and for the great deal of you who I may never meet who long to live a life both free and fulfilled. Not one that is devoid of the trials and vicissitudes we all must face that come to make us stronger. But a life that consists of the fulfillment that comes from living in line with who you were always meant to be – a life that consists of the inner peace that is experienced when you realize that you are becoming the person of your dreams and don't care what others think about it. I want to empower both the person who struggles within themselves and others because they don't fit in, and the person who struggles within themselves and with others because all they do is try to fit in. Some of you are both in one.

Many of you will be enlightened to the fact that you were in a fight that you never realized you were in – that the frustration and uneasiness that has lead some of you to anxiety, depression and hopelessness is not just the result of a job, a set of friends or a particular environment. But it's "finding your place" that has exhausted your mind and your members and has caused your soul to become restless. It isn't external at all. Sometimes it's the detrimental result of attempting to run someone else's race, winded by an unrelenting jealousy and need for validation, causing you to compete with others in order to find self-worth, that has you against the ropes of life…but we'll talk about that and more later on. Let's go.

A New Home

I. Mistake

AS FOR ME, I wouldn't have realized it then but the people around me should have definitely seen the direction my life was going in from the very beginning. Even at birth, I had a case of mistaken Identity. It's a story that comes up every now and then amongst my immediate family. You see, I had very little color in my skin when I was born, and that became a problem when it was time for guests to view me through the nursery window. Evidently, my grandparents, who are African-American, and a white couple, were both standing outside of the nursery. My grandmother and grandfather had both already been at the hospital for a while but the other couple had just gotten there to see their new family member for the first time. The problem was that when the white couple asked, eagerly I'm sure, to see the child that belonged to their family, the nurse looked around and without checking any of our wrist tags, decided that I was the child that most looked like he fit with them. There couldn't have been very many babies to choose from. The nurse then reaches into the acrylic, transparent bin the hospital labeled a crib, lifts me up and walks me over to the viewing window right in front of the couple. Imagine being the grandparents of the child that was about to be "given away" to a completely different family – of a completely different race! Fortunately, my grandmother, who I affectionately call Nana, had already come to see me once by herself and immediately spotted the mistake that was being made. She called out to the nurse saying "Hey! That's my grandbaby!" To her surprise, the nurse then argumentatively looks back at her as if there was no way my grandmother knew what she was talking about. She was certain that I could not have belonged to my grandparents based upon my pigmentation. "Check the tag!" my grandma insisted. The nurse then reluctantly checked the name on my wrist and let out an embarrassed "Ohhhhh". Shaking her head, she then apologized to the other couple and proceeded to put me back and get the right baby. I guess it was a sign that people might just get me wrong my entire life.

II. Bus Passes And Fashion Sense

Reflecting on what I can remember, I'm actually shocked at how many bouts with fitting in I had to have before I realized that...I didn't. It's really not until I take a retrospective look that I realize how much I never really did. Not to sound unaware or to toot my own horn, but I don't know that I've been one to analyze my differences from others that much. I've actually even been one to pride myself on "seeing no color" and all that other admirable, unifying stuff we say that, at best, is normally only partially true. Of course I can actually see color and differences but I've had a best friend who is white for the majority of my life for goodness' sake. I'm "black" by the way. And to be honest, accounting the fact that we both went to all of the same schools (Elementary, Middle and High School) and that those schools were probably never less than 49% black, I'm pretty sure he's as close to being culturally "black" as I am. But in all seriousness, I can honestly say this: I really never dishonored anyone's "difference". From an early age, I had even been drawn to the weird, introverted and overlooked - the "different" ones. I can still remember the faces and some of the names of certain people I made it my goal to see laugh before we left class. There was something about their reserved demeanor and "crouched" disposition, as if to hide themselves amongst other people that made me want to let them know that I saw them. Maybe that's because underneath the threads of what my mom would describe as my "expensive taste", I was the same as they were: someone that didn't fit in.

On the surface, it was probably pretty obvious from an outside perspective to see that I didn't fit in. I used to be too shy to even want to. I can still remember my comfortable yet nerve-racking car rides to school during my elementary days. I was unwilling to ride the bus, due to my severe shyness of course. And of course because of the severity of my issue, I was also unwilling to be seen as a "car-rider". The tension was monstrous. I'll never forget secretly hoping we wouldn't pass or even come close to the bus I would've been riding had I not been so deathly

A New Home

afraid. The days when I didn't have to see a bus at all (I doubt that there were many) were the greatest. I could even survive if there were three or more cars in-between us. The kicker was when I had to actually face the fear of being seen, which happened on a regular basis. Don't worry, I figured out a way to avoid overcoming that fear all together. It was called hiding. If we were behind a bus, that was the easiest. Being in elementary school, I was still a pretty small guy. All I had to do was bend at the waist slowly so that the seatbelt wouldn't lock (I learned that the hard way) and disappear behind the dashboard. Poof! All of a sudden, my mom was alone, driving herself to my school for some apparent reason. That's what I wanted everyone to think at least. The most difficult position to play my disappearing act in was directly beside the bus. You see, no one wants to be stuck behind a bus during drop-offs and pick-ups, especially in the small town of Salisbury, North Carolina where there were very few four-lane roads. Neither did my mom. So if she ever got the chance, she'd attempt to pass it. Sometimes that meant us being stuck at a stoplight right beside my arch-nemesis: a bus full of my scary peers. I can only imagine how interesting it would be for an eight-year-old to glance down from the elevated vantage point of a school bus through the window of my mom's Honda Accord, only to see a boy fully crouched between her cloth seats and leather dashboard. For some reason, I actually thought my technique worked! So much so, that it was my "go to" every time the same predicament occurred.

Listen, before you get all judgmental, you have to understand the severity of my issue. If you were under the same stress, you might have done worse. I'm going to go out on a limb and say you would have! I'm sure you can imagine the ups and downs throughout the rest of my school day. That was just the car ride there.

My entire youth was filled with some of those same ups and downs. I progressively got over some of my fears of course. Some of that came with maturity and I accredit some of it to what I'll call "the more

A New Home

popular parts of myself". You see, sometimes you get a pass on an "interesting personality" when you have a little talent, decent looks and impeccable fashion sense. Let's just agree that that's factual. Although they came natural to me, those "likable attributes" became a mask of sorts to the shy, introverted, seemingly less relatable portions of me. I would be considered a smart, cool, artistic guy who could even get some "best dressed" class superlative votes to some on one hand, but the encounters that required me to interact with others on a more personal level were entirely different. Let's call the close quarter attributes the "underdeveloped attributes". If I named them from an insider's perspective, they were more like "the attributes that I could care less about". I didn't mind them being underdeveloped then and although I do care about personal growth, I still don't at all mind being an introvert to this day. It's who I am.

Although I've constantly been around people my entire life, I don't have too many recollections of those up-close and personal encounters from my early days to share with you because, as I've stated, I didn't always desire to have them in the first place. As a matter of fact, I'm certain that, from what I've heard and have been directly told, at least 90% of the people around me at any point then probably had no idea I could talk. That's just an educated guess. Most people have kept that record of me both inside and outside of school my entire life. Here's what I can tell you about those encounters though; for the most part, if my mouth wasn't sealed, it was getting me in trouble. From report-card notes, to reprimands, to being fired when I was older and everything in-between, I've experienced a range of consequences for a certain outspokenness over my lifetime. I've managed to do some good with these teeth by now, but in my early years, those times were few and far-between.

III. Temporary Blindness

Now, if you've been tracking with me this far, you might be wondering "How in the world could you not realize you "didn't exactly fit in" with a history like that?!"…The answer is latent within everything I just described to you about my past.

First, I'm an introvert. Here's a quick psychological definition of introversion: "a person characterized by concern primarily with his or her own thoughts and feelings". Basically, it's: "a person so fascinated with their own thoughts and feelings that the outside world often takes a back seat to their inward show". That's my personal rendition of a clinical definition. That factor alone could cause you to miss out so much happening around you. And now that I think about it, that "selective memory" my wife's been complaining about should probably be accredited to my introvert nature.

Secondly, I was kind-of cool. A few compliments every now and then from the outside world could hold someone over with my personality type for a while; considering that I was in my own world most of the time of course.

I had also accumulated several academic and extracurricular awards (the nerdy kind) and even received the class superlative entitled "Most Likely to Succeed" once. Go figure. And I didn't even have to speak to anyone to get it! I was just as flabbergasted about that one as you may be! And not to mention highly flattered. But even then, those moments kept a quiet confidence brewing on the inside that blinded me from the reality of my situation.

I should probably accredit it to a great family dynamic too. I was able to grow up with a good number of immediate family members who were all close to my age and therefore shared many commonalities. I don't think I considered fit as much when it came to family, especially in my youth. This is primarily because no one gets to choose his or her family. In the beginning, how you fit isn't even a consideration. You have to.

A New Home

As it is with everyone, much of my family dynamic is actually what shaped my perspective and honestly affected my fit on the outside to a large extent. And because some of us were so close growing up, based upon our ideals of what love and family was, I was spared of not having and place to call home concerning fitting in because fitting in concerning family just didn't matter at the time. Again, it wasn't even a consideration. Forced and wanted interaction mixed with the innocence of young sibling-like family love literally blocked that dynamic out for the most part. From my experience, fit doesn't necessarily play an undeniably visible part in family life until everyone grows up and becomes responsible for making their own decisions apart from the instructions of their parents or guardians. And those then visible differences themselves are what often show fit in family life.

You can imagine how discombobulating those factors alone could be to finding your fit. On one hand, I didn't care to fit at all and yet, somehow on the other hand, in certain situations, I still did.

Bryan Pharr

Wanting to avoid all awkward social situations and stay to myself had pretty much taught me how to spend most days practically unnoticed. And when I was noticed, I had "the more popular attributes" to cover for me. I never used fashion sense and "swag" to cover myself intentionally. Those parts were just as genuine as the shy, introverted parts. The interesting thing for me is that somehow both the "popular" and underdeveloped sides collaborated to keep me under the radar. My being shy was an asset in that it kept me out of the upper echelon of popularity and placed me more toward the "misunderstood" category. My coolness on the other hand, kept me away from the misunderstood and from the bullies that would sometimes torment them so. I could almost say I was in an entire category of my own. I wouldn't have said that at the time.

I guess ONE upside to all of this would be that, for the most part, my existence then was drama free. That's if you don't count what was going on internally at times. No detentions, expulsions or arrests from unlawful peer interactions. It wasn't

A New Home

until later on in life that I realized the sort of mess I was in; "not fitting in".

Bryan Pharr

Imagination is everything. It is the preview of life's coming attractions.

– **Albert Einstein**

IV. Dreamweaver

I suppose one of the greatest assets, and sometimes disadvantages of being under the radar as an introvert, is the freedom to constantly DREAM. For me, this was almost a way of life. I could, and still can, daydream at any moment. Whether surrounded by a room filled with people or even in mid conversation, nothing can deter these visual thoughts from whimsically drawing my attention away from the outside world. To date, I can often find my attention playing tug-of-war with this alternate reality just long enough to have a decent, uninterrupted conversation; or to write this book for that matter. As disruptive as all of this may sound, I can't say that I would trade the ability for a thing. I honestly believe it's the place where the God-dreams that inform my mission and

A New Home

purpose are born to form my reality; a connector of sorts between what's not yet and what is.

Growing up, I probably didn't recognize it as much of a "gift". It was just normal. All day, every day, I could be found whisked away into my own imagination. Growing up as an only child at home gave me countless hours to contribute to my habit. And it often resulted in class-long art sessions or restless behavior in school. Once, I even had a girl next to me in my elementary class laughing uncontrollably at what had become a two person stage play scene that I was acting out aloud all by myself.

I should note that although my grades remained pretty good at the time, these were things that normally got me in trouble and were often noted by the teacher under those good grades on my report cards.

I had an imagination that would run wild and I couldn't stop it. Nor did I want to. It was my escape from whatever boring lesson my teachers were teaching at the moment and from the inherent loneliness of being in a single-child home. Super Mario, Sonic the Hedgehog and a plethora of other video game and television characters were constantly entertaining me on a daily basis early on.

As I grew older, my dreams of being in a "Disney-World" with all of my favorite characters soon turned to dreaming of working at Disney World as an "Imagineer" and a host of other dreams that are appealing to a certain type of growing mind; like being a scientist, astronaut, fireman, or something else adventurous. At certain points in time, I wanted to be all of these. I suppose I fit in with many youth my age pertaining to that matter, being that many of these are the dreams normally fed to young minds as possible career options.

Alongside those dreams there seemed to be a different stream of ideas that were eventually being born from my instincts. They were what I call the more "realistic" dreams. This is not to say that these dreams were at all small. They were just dreams that made perfect sense based on how, I can now say, I'm

A New Home

designed or wired as person. They catered to my personal gifts/abilities/talents and calling. They were accompanied by a strong desire within me and gave me a sense of purpose and a drive before I really recognized my own purpose or even understood what purpose was in general. I guess a good way to describe the feeling is that these thoughts and ideas stirred something within; an uncompromising determination. Even to the point that some of my teenage dreams and visions haven't loosed their hold on me to this day. It is almost as if, in part, they were implanted by God Himself.

These dreams were tangible. I believe this was the key factor that set them apart from some of the fairytale imaginations I had in previous years. And this would be another reason to describe them as realistic. They involved other real people and not just the characters from my Saturday morning cartoon connection or the vivid scenes painted by great storytellers in the books I had to read in order to get a free personal-pan pizza every now and then. The intent behind them was to make the world a better place for certain people I had a burden for and therefore gave responsibility, depth and meaning to what otherwise could have just been a dream or an escape.

Please understand. I am in no way saying that it was the fairytale nature of my adolescent dreams that made them less realistic. I THANK GOD for the great artists, inventors, and creators that connected us to their wonder-worlds. Time spent immersed in their creations make for euphoric and sometimes thought-provoking experiences that dare us to dream our own dreams. It's just that at the time, it wasn't my intent to connect others to what I envisioned. They were just self-involved dreams and escapes...from boring classes and sometimes just from reality...harmless, but not exactly helpful to others. It wasn't until I matured a little and began to see some of the things going on in the world from a different perspective that my dreams became ones that would connect me with what was happening around me; dreams that I believed could better the worlds of others around me.

A New Home

I can honestly say that I count not fitting in concerning this matter as more of an advantage than a disadvantage. I had ample time to mentally develop "alone" without getting caught in the peer pressures of my day and like some, be solely focused on or highly occupied with the constantly changing trends. I was able to develop a decent worldview. I partly accredit that to my upbringing of course. It caused me to grow up in some areas a little faster although the tension to fall into normal teenage traps was there eventually also. There are certain things that hormones and puberty just don't allow you to intellectualize your way out of. A growing interest in girls and relationships can definitely throw a couple complications in the life of a young boy who is comfortable in darn-near isolation. But more than anything else, the ability to grow and think without the permission or influence of those around me would be something that would later serve me more than hurt me. I can assure you though, that it has done both.

Fear and faith are both imaginary. Fear is just the imagination [uncontrolled]

– Tony Robbins

V. Dark Fantasies

As with everything in life, "there are two sides to every coin". I mentioned earlier that not fitting into a specific "category" or group of people during my school years made me feel as if I had mistakenly been put in a category of my own. But what may not have been apparent about that statement is the inherent dark side of being in that type of position. Loneliness, unwarranted thoughts, self-suppression and slight embarrassment at times were all constant, felt emotions of being in my reality. Even having a strong imagination can work against you if those thoughts aren't controlled. It has the ability to paint a gorgeous paradise or an elaborate hell over the same narrative.

Let's talk about the loneliness for a moment. This is probably the most obvious and expected

A New Home

symptom of being a black sheep. Not feeling as if there is anyone who could relate to where you are is not only a valid feeling based from facts at times, it's also the result of being in "your own world" and not realizing that there are more people than you know who are experiencing the same things right around you at other times. Although all of our stories are different, I've realized now, more than ever, that chances are, there's probably at least one person with a similar story near you at all times. This ultimately let's me know that this kind of suffering is not without purpose but becomes the very testimony that allows someone else to overcome their adversities.

But let's face it. Loneliness sucks, testimony or not. Especially when you aren't mature enough to even know that the pain of it can be turned into purpose. At the time, it just feels like pain. Or if you're like me, at other times, just a hiding place to conceal the full version of you or else risk sticking out.

Bryan Pharr

The irony for me was that either way, I was going to. Being "alone" in plain sight doesn't exactly always take attention from you. Luckily, I was always blessed with at least two friends that I could talk to and family that would keep me from constantly being somewhat isolated. But they couldn't always be there. Weekdays spent in a single parent/single child home often left me alone in my room wishing to God that my mom would somehow conceive a little girl so that I could have a baby sister to spend time with. Not sharing classes or breaks with friends often left me sitting at lunch tables, in classes or standing in hallways in high school alone.

This was often the source of my embarrassment – sitting at lunch tables and standing in halls in high school alone, that is. Being in those positions and also being fully aware of the possible and sometimes-actual major attention being drawn to me for it was almost unbearable. Noticing people notice me and possibly base an unknown conversation from it, while having to pretend that I didn't notice them and simultaneously act as if I'm cool with it was

A New Home

the worst. You can imagine how much quicker I finished lunch and scurried out of the cafeteria than others when this alone time lasted longer than I could handle.

Though you may be able to be empathetic, I'm sure this sounds quite stupid to many of you. But the truth is that it was my reality. It was almost as if, to me, the pain of sticking out within a group for being my authentic self and possibly being rejected for it was still less than the embarrassment of not even trying to fit in at all. The best times were when the table I was sitting at alone filled up with other people out of necessity because the other tables were already full. There were also a couple times that a decent hearted person who honestly either just felt bad for me, secretly liked me or didn't understand why I was sitting there alone would invite me to sit with them and their friends. This definitely alleviated the embarrassment for the moment and actually made me feel as if I fit. And I kind of did. As long as I was quiet, still hiding behind the silence, so I thought.

The rest of the times, I was at the mercy of my speed, my ability to "hide", my ability to "not care" and my ability to use my imagination.

Two of the more interesting effects of introversion are that, not only do you formulate conclusions about yourself internally, but you can also have a tendency to formulate other people's conclusions about you without their involvement. This isn't necessarily the effect of being non-confrontational, which is sometimes the case. For me, it was just another effect of not wanting to come out of hiding and not caring enough to go out of my way to find out. One thing that I admittedly have been wrong about on multiple occasions throughout my life is my perception of what certain people have thought about me. It's a dangerous game to play. If you aren't accurate and wise, you could potentially damage a good thing before it even happens. Here's what I mean: It's popularly said that assumptions (have the ability to) make an "ass" out of you and me. ASS-U-ME. This isn't only true within established relationships. It's also true of possible relationships.

A New Home

We all do it. We forfeit the opportunity of what could be life-changing experiences and relationships based upon our assumptions of others that don't allow us to even entertain the possibility at all. It isn't that we shouldn't use sound judgment when it comes to our affiliations. But ignorant prejudice, irrational paranoia and/or personal insecurities shouldn't be the basis by which we decide whom we will connect with.

I had a habit of making the same type of assumptions but in reverse. It's how I began to realize that rejection isn't just an experience that other people can put you through. It's also a prison you can decide to keep yourself in. The same imagination that kept me entertained while I was "bored spit-less" in certain classes, was the same force that pre-determined how bothered people would be by me if they experienced an uninhibited Bryan. I wasn't this way in my early days when I was continuously called out for my restless behavior and talkative nature. It's amazing how one or two instances of rejection or disapproval can change the trajectory of your entire social life if you allow it to.

Bryan Pharr

It happened to me in the sixth grade. I'll never forget it. I was sitting in a math class with my colleagues and the teacher presented us with a difficult problem that she intended for us to solve while she went to the front office to take care of some unknown business of her own. Wanting to have a unanimous, correct answer by the time the teacher returned, everyone discussed his or her calculations and answers aloud. There were only two of us who had come up with a different answer than the rest. I was one of them. Math, a subject that I would grow to hate in the coming years was actually one of my favorite courses at the time, so I was very confident in the answer I had come up with. The opposing answer in the room gained much of its strength from the amount of people who all agreed that it was the accurate resolution. They were just as sure. A neighboring girl who shared the same solution as me was insistent upon drawing out her calculations on the white board for everyone to see after it became apparent that neither side was willing give up their position. Even after that final plea in illustration form,

A New Home

there still remained only the two of us with an opposing answer. After all, even if they were unsure, who would have switched "teams" with odds like that?

Those odds made me come alive. I was so certain of my result that I would have argued it to the teacher if it came down to it. The bigger the giant, sweeter the victory. I was all in to prove that what the girl and I were going to present was the actual right solution. My loud, passionate attempts to convince my classmates of my mathematics along with her tactical presentation weren't working and I was excited about it! I couldn't wait to "kick everyone while they were down" after finding out they were wrong by saying "I told you so". So much so that I actually did it when the teacher returned and everyone found out that we were right. I was overjoyed! But what happened next was completely unexpected. Another young lady to my immediate left promptly let me know how she felt about my proud display of being on the winning side with a violent "SHUT UP"! She proceeded to tell me in short words how much she disliked the fact that I was right. It was as if I had tapped a well of deep, bottled frustration within her.

What she didn't know was that her reaction would become the basis for a long span of silence within my educational experience, because I had decided that I wasn't going to allow "who I was" to annoy anyone else. After all, how was I supposed to help the fact that math was a subject that excited me and that I was good at? That's how I thought about it at the time anyway. And all jokes aside, I really hadn't intended to do any harm to anyone with any display of happiness over correctly solving a middle school math problem. I had been labeled a "motor mouth" and as restless by a couple of teachers a number of times before that day. I had even been punched in the face for telling a joke that the young girl I told it to obviously didn't like. But it all seemed to have culminated in that single moment. That was the last straw. I no longer wanted to offend or annoy anyone with "who I was". I began to live in a state of rejection, always making their decision for them by assuming that others wouldn't like me if I opened up.

A New Home

These assumptions were normally backed by realistic reasons why, such as, "they won't understand or receive me as one of them because I don't do what they do, say what they say, have what they have" or sometimes even "believe what they believe". Because of the conclusion I had drawn, that imagination that I loved so dearly had turned against me when it came to my interactions with others. I had already drawn out the failure of a relational pursuit many times before it even started. And the expectancy of that rejection kept me to myself most days and though now based from a more keen discernment, it still can in certain situations today honestly.

Just to be clear, I don't believe every part of my conclusion was wrong. Again, I wouldn't have explained it this way then, but more than anything, this was the moment that I began to accept my difference – the fact that I didn't fit in. And let's be honest. The reasons listed above, not to mention socioeconomic status, racial identification and a slew of other categorizations, are the ACTUAL substratum by which many of us reject one another today. It became obvious to me through many experiences that what I chose to do and say were often dramatically different than what others chose. There were many more instances beyond this one that would come to prove my initial hypothesis. Life became about whether I would pay the cost of expressing my difference or choose to hide, attempting to avoid that cost all together. Luckily, those were the only two options I had. It's the same choice we all have to make sooner or later. I believe many of us add a third option in our lives though. The third option would be to bend or change in order to fit in with others. I don't want to lead you to think that it was me that I had the problem with. I liked me. I loved my interests, hobbies, gifts and personality. Even through moments of insecurity about my looks formed from being picked on by various "bullies", I never wanted to change who I was. I enjoyed me. The problem was that I didn't quite know who else would, and soon began to think that there wouldn't be very many who did. I felt that, just maybe, I'd have to experience a certain type of loneliness my entire life. Choosing to

A New Home

stay quiet from a combination of being shy and knowing I was "different" left me simply having to imagine what others thought about me rather than having a clear revelation. And unfortunately, because of a few bad experiences, those imaginings often drew a negative perception. It was the beginning of what was probably a small loss of hope in other people concerning myself and maybe an insecurity or lack of confidence in whether there would be many others who saw me the way I did.

VI. Lost

This dilemma attributed to what was probably the most difficult and long lasting obstacle to navigate. As much as I can say that all of these things actually added to the process of self-discovery, at the time it didn't seem like it at all. If anything, the journey to identity and purpose for me became a long road to navigate rather than a short one due to the fact that I didn't have many relationships to gain insight from. I've mainly had to gain insight through the negative experiences I've had rather than just having someone positively affect me with affirmations, confirmation or by pouring out the mystical knowledge some of you'd expect to receive after seeking out a prophet, or for others, calling a psychic hotline. By now, I've had some of those positive affirmations and confirmation. But, for the most part, taking the type of deep, analytical, introspective looks at myself that it takes to write these pages, mixed with the same type of investigative, retrospective looks at

A New Home

the varying experiences I have had throughout my life collectively have helped the most.

Like many others, thoughts of personal identity and purpose didn't hit me hard until I began to have to think about what direction I thought my life should go in. I believe it's difficult enough to make those types of discoveries and decisions as a teenager or a young adult for anyone. Especially if you're a part of an educational system that does not deploy any form of self-awareness training or actually cater to ALL career options by speaking directly to the gifts and abilities within ALL children. I am not saying that this would be an easy task. Nor am I saying that it's the primary function of the educational system to bring about this self-awareness and direction to children. This foundation HAS to be a priority of parents in the homes of every child and a taught personal responsibility of every child. But here's what I know: Even as a child who was rightfully invested in musically by my parents, which has brought me significant fulfillment and opportunity, there were still other gifts within me that remained practically dormant and untapped for a while. This was partially because of being raised overall within a single parent structure.

There are two beliefs I hold that will testify to that statement. The first is that "the apple never falls far from the tree". What I am implying here is that many of the gifts and abilities I have can easily be traced somewhere within my lineage. For instance, I stated that music is a gift of mine that has given a lot back to me. Well, both my mother and my father are musicians in their own right. My mother sings to this day and my dad plays multiple instruments. A couple of my grandparents are also musicians. The problem was that being raised singly only gave me an "up close and personal" view of one parent's gifts and inclinations initially, which ultimately, assuming my ideology is correct, made it more difficult to have a full perspective of my own potential. As a side note, what this first ideology also implies is that not seeing my parents fully walk out their purposes and use all of their gifts, would also limit my ability to see my own purpose and gifts.

A New Home

The second belief I have is that it is the gifting of a father to impart identity. It's probably self-explanatory why this could cause a bit of added difficulty for me to fully know who I was and gain a strong sense of purpose early on. But that subject, in its entirety, is also for another book.

I also have to mention that the immediate family I was raised under, though all great people, as a whole wasn't particularly big on the ideas of intentional affirmation, building a strong sense of identity and "fully and confidently walking out your unique purpose to see your destiny" in general. My mother, even in our relationship at times was just as quiet as I was, if not more. After getting older and beginning to conceive those "realistic dreams", I often found myself vacant of the affirmation and vote of confidence that I THOUGHT I needed from her or others in order to pursue those big goals. For us, it just wasn't a thing. And truthfully, no one can pass along what they hadn't received. It wasn't an established pattern within our family.

Now, on top of all of these, were the facts that I didn't fit in with any particular crowd and that I had already began to loose hope in having relationships with most people as an adolescent from encountering rejection and simply not fitting in. What this would essentially come to mean, as I got older, is that being conscious of the reality that I didn't fit in would not necessarily indicate that I knew why. This is because I still wasn't quite clear on who I was. My experience in effect consisted of many cycles of starting over and over simply because I had no or very little idea of, and confidence in, the direction I should go. I fell into a lifestyle for a while that so many of us do throughout this world that I'll describe as "living lost". It's possible to live a life filled with an appearance of victory and success while never actually seeing maximum fulfillment as a result of not fully living out who you were meant to be. It's possible to have a lucrative career and be well taken care of without ever intentionally using your gifts or manifesting your dream. But for me, this wasn't living at all. I had seen stages, lights, thousands of people and even been on

A New Home

television internationally as a musician before the age of thirty (I'm currently still under thirty years of age). #Goals, right? What's amazing is that I was still left feeling unfulfilled concerning the dreams and gifts I knew were left untapped. I should also mention that, by now, I have been fired from a significant amount of jobs and am a repeat college dropout. These are some of the telltale signs that ultimately let me know that I wasn't quite in tact with who I was and therefore not able to live at a complete place of purpose and fulfillment.

Because I only had a limited perspective of the type of value I could bring people, due to a lack of gained experience through the relationships I might have pursued had I not doubted humanity, the dreams that I had to help or inspire others would often become clouded as a result of an absence of clarity concerning how I would actually do it. The easiest way for anyone to become confused about a goal, dream, idea or his or her purpose is to not step out on it. In the same way, as long as I was accepting of the rejected, introvert, black sheep role, I could only gain a certain amount of awareness and practice concerning my other gifts, which my dreams ultimately depended on. You see, it's much more difficult to discover a gift of gab if you don't ever talk. Similarly, gifts of leadership, counsel, or any other gifts that involve other people are pretty hard to recognize within yourself if you're cooped up in your own world. Again, it's not that I hadn't experienced rejection, wasn't naturally an introvert, or couldn't technically classify myself as a black sheep. But my perception of those realities would ultimately shape my world. Choosing to hide due to being shy, timid or "living rejected" had proven to make a difficult situation even more difficult. It's almost as if hiding from others meant hiding myself from me. I find that as many enemies as there are possible to have, the biggest one you can have is you, if you allow yourself to be. My unwillingness to be free and be noticed became the very thing that kept me in the dark concerning my place in this world. It was a double-edged sword. On one hand, being quiet and reserved meant a lack of fulfillment and purpose. And on the

A New Home

other hand, for a while, I thought opening my mouth or openly being myself meant only being rejected. I had no idea that this nightmare of a reality could be the very thing that transported me to a place of realized identity and fulfillment.

The Interlude

Just in case you're beginning to think this book is entirely about my childhood, let me assure you that it's not...completely. I would never write a book that only encompassed my boring yet somehow dramatic adolescent years. If you need a break from all of the DRAMA, by all means, take 5 minutes; make yourself some coffee or tea and come right back. I'm building a case here.

Chapter II:

TRANSIT

VII. Wave Runner

Let me start this section, not by framing an outlook on transition, but by framing a perspective of life itself. I'm certain that this brief synopsis will fall dramatically (and intentionally) short of a full "master's overview" from God, found coded within sacred text. But it is not my aim to answer all of your questions about life in one chapter of this book. Today, I am only making it my job to outline the way I see life working for two categories of people: sinkers and swimmers. I think we just about all fit into one or the other.

It fascinates me that the same properties and attributes of water that so many people grow fond of

A New Home

are the same properties and attributes that others learn to fear and avoid. Consider in your mind a pool or an ocean. Isn't it amazing that the same aquatic environment that many barely survive in and some die in, others thrive in? How could it be that what is seen as a foe to many also be considered a friend to many others? To some, it's a place of refreshing and relaxation but to others, a death wish waiting to be fulfilled. To numerous athletes, it's a training ground used to their advantage. Others will never know its training advantages. To some, it is a tool made FOR them. They ride its waves for enjoyment and experiment with its properties to see how it can benefit their lives. Others see it as a force bent AGAINST them, opposing the ease and enjoyment they so desire.

It has been my observation that this is the way most people see and experience life. We're either sinkers or swimmers in it. We either feel like it's a tool given FOR our fulfillment or a force set AGAINST our comfort and peace. I would suggest that how see your life will determine how your shape your life. Either you will be excited about it, welcoming all of its waves and attributes for your ultimate enjoyment or you will fear and dread it daily, waiting on "the next bad thing" to happen. It shapes whether you enjoy your days and their challenges or whether you live them out in pain. It determines whether you live openly, having a hopeful expectation of the future or whether you are closed and depressed, only counting the days until you die. It is the basis for whether you view life as a punishment we all have to go through until you hopefully meet a better day in an expected after-life or whether you face all of life's challenges and ride its waves with an assured expectation of heaven on earth.

It's also the lens by which you determine why things happen to you. It determines whether you see that car wreck, sickness or event that you were a victim of, as, again, either punishment, or, for swimmers, as guidance. This is in no way diminishing the magnitude of pain that can come from some of the unfortunate circumstances and happenings all of us

A New Home

face, but rather emphasizing our ability to choose our view of them.

Most of you have learned to choose the first option as your default perspective. Life, for you, is an adversary. Every attempt to settle and get comfortable in a routine you can handle always seems to be met with another one of life's waves that catch you off guard and come to take you under. "Life's a b@&#h!" If there is a God, you believe he hates you and has cursed you by bringing you into this world. You can't seem to win from loosing. Life for you isn't an ocean. It's quicksand. And even your attempts to fight your way out are only burying you deeper. You've resolved to barely live with regard for others, if any at all – not to mention any regard for yourself. "Why shouldn't I just overdose on my "drug" of choice until it all goes away? Why not end it all? No one cares about me anyway! What's the purpose of this life anyway? Why shouldn't I cut corners, steal and cheat to get what I want? "They'll" have it better off regardless. Who gives a s%*@# about them? They're all against me! This whole world is going to hell, so why does it matter anyway?" This is the logic of a sinker. It drives every decision and informs every "why" you ever ask. This is learned thought and behavior gained from negative circumstances and negative influences. You're without hope. Your entire goal in life is comfort.

This is entirely different from the swimmer – the wave runner. Being met with the SAME adversity or worse only exposes opportunity for you. Every wave that life sends your way, no matter the size, does not come to take you under. It comes to expose and prove you. To you, they come to expose the god in every one of us. You ride them with an expectation of greater at their end. Your goal is growth. You live with purpose and intent. You're aware of the tools that were given to you for your success – your gifts/talents and capacity (or potential). You realize that the universe itself is bent in your favor should you choose to believe so. You recognize that every wave of adversity breeds lessons and directions that are FOR you, not against you. Because you hold yourself in high regard, you also regard the lives of

A New Home

others highly. You too learned and adopted this thought and behavior. In time, you've discovered the ease and flow that comes when you learn not to fight against or waste time and energy trying to wish away the water and its waves that hold you afloat. Instead you learned to overcome and ride them to your next and greater destination.

I want to submit to you that in both cases the water is the same. It has the same properties and attributes. Sure, maybe you were born in a region where the weather is different; the water is colder or the storms may seem to be more often and torrential. But here's the secret the swimmer knows: No matter the size or consistency of the storms in your life, there's nothing more powerful than what's IN you and what's FOR you. Storms only come to prove that the strength to overcome them is there. So again, no matter the waters, it's your perspective and power that make all the difference. We ALL have the option and grace to be wave runners.

VIII. Back to Back

I needed to frame my perspective of life for you before diving into my personal experiences because, for me, it has been both a foe and a friend. To be 100% honest and clear, I had to learn to only view it as a friend over time. It wasn't just blatantly understood for me at first. This was especially true when circumstances were torrential. It seems as if I've been through just about "a little of everything" by this point. At first, I didn't understand the value that experience could bring to your life. While going through hard times, it just seems like everything is working against you. It takes time to realize that everything was working for you. The reason why it takes time is because you have to live to see what's on the other side of those circumstances or trials.

I would eventually begin to see those tough times as a means of transit or transportation. Just as described earlier, it was those "waves" that life brought, whether large and horrific or just inconvenient and uncomfortable, that were actually

A New Home

serving as directed transit to take me to a greater destination. Beyond my obviously interesting childhood, I've faced plenty of rejection, being outcast and fired from multiple jobs. I've found discontent with school (college) from what I consider was a lack of knowing who I was and as a result, have gone and dropped out at least five times (from five different schools). In retrospect, I would also accredit the ever-eventual disinterest with my schooling to the entrepreneur in me that would quickly grow bored with indoctrination and a lack of the type of education that would feed my actual interests and instincts. I went through years of sickness, including more hospital visits and stays than I can remember across the state of North Carolina, trying to identify an unknown and seemingly incurable "dis-ease". I've faced the challenges of these waves and more only to discover that they would be the very vehicles that would lift my perspective, show my strength, and reveal to me who I am. They also gave me something to say. It was the waves that shaped who I am and brought me from everything I described earlier to where I am today. They've made me a bona fide wave runner.

But as I stated before, I didn't always have the knowledge and wisdom to be able to see what was happening. I couldn't just peacefully ride those waves with an assurance of things only getting better, no matter how hard it was at the time. At first it just seemed like hell. I felt the way so many of you may even feel right now. It seemed as if the waves just wouldn't stop coming. Any attempt to even believe that I could find stability, long-term comfort or even alliance would soon be met with another wave to tear the hope down.

Believe me. There were some beautiful moments throughout those years too. For instance, I came in contact with a godsend of a woman who would eventually end every belief and concern that I had about having to do life alone. She's my wife. But even she was just someone I could confide in at the time and find comfort in while the waves continued to

A New Home

come. Later, through marriage, she was the one who was "anointed" to ride the waves with me.

I'll never forget calling her after conversing with God one day while we were still dating. That was a normal practice for me, but trust me, the right amount of difficulty will have ANYONE recognizing or calling on God, whether questioning or cursing. I called her crying hysterically because, what I felt like I got out of the conversation was that the waves weren't going to stop coming – true story. I felt as if the circumstances around me weren't going to change and that the amount of waves weren't going to decrease. And they didn't. Wave after wave, they wouldn't let up. Drake's "Back to Back" was the soundtrack of my life at the time, but in a bad way. I was the one taking the "L's" (losses) left and right. What I didn't understand then was that as long as there was somewhere for me to go and to grow, they wouldn't stop coming.

I should stop here and let you know that it's the same for you too. Remember that life's challenges or waves are just a means of transit. As long as you have somewhere further to go or some way to grow, you can count on the waves coming. No one is exempt. What's important is that you learn how to see those waves. In your mind they'll either be adversaries to your comfort or allies of your destiny. The choice is yours. But they won't stop coming. The truth is, change is not your enemy. Difficulty is not your enemy. Loss is not your enemy. Again, I am not diminishing the pain that can come from any difficult situation. But these things can be the very vehicles that grow you and strengthen you should you choose to see them as such and endure with hopeful expectation. The quickest way to continuously get ran over and live a sinkers lifestyle is to decide that you'll fight against what's holding you up – what's transporting you. The entire universe is bent towards your win. I'm challenging you to find out what's in you and learn to ride those waves. You weren't made to become a victim of your circumstances. You were made to rise above them.

A New Home

I heard someone say to someone else before, "Your arms are too short to box with God". The way I interpreted that phrase was that, in the waters and waves of life, you either ride or die. If you're in this world, the waves are coming – sometimes inconvenient and most of the time, unannounced. There's a flow and a current to your life that is meant to push you toward your destiny. It doesn't stop. And to resist it means to die. And trust me, you don't have to be in your grave to be dead. Living the life of a sinker, fearful, anxious, depressed and hopeless, is death. It's conscious death. I want you to live the life of a swimmer so that no matter the difficulty, you can face the challenge with both confidence and peace through the pain. And here's the hope: with every wave, you're being pushed through another threshold of strength, confidence, self-awareness and stamina. Before you know it, the waves that would knock you completely off balance and have you in an emotional frenzy for months on end in your early "riding years" will be the very waves that you will eventually put to shame with your wave-riding abilities. You'll be able to laugh at the adversity that used to make you cry. You'll be able to face that same rejection, that same loss, that same hate, and that same trouble with a strength and tenacity that leads to resounding triumph. You won't have to suffer the waves always. They'll keep coming. But before long, you'll become so strong that the waves will have to begin to suffer you. This is the inheritance of the wave runner. It's the prize of the person who chooses to believe that those waves don't come to take you under. They come to take you higher and further than you've ever been before. The bigger the waves, the greater the destination.

A New Home

"Brief Origin Story"

This book is based from a four-part video, visual monologue I made and released in 2016 entitled "A New Home". You can still find it on YouTube today. Within it, I illustrate and vaguely narrate many of the events that brought me to where I am today. In "Chapter III" (the third video), I describe the exact transition my "waves" have taken me through thus far. For me it has been a journey of self-discovery (Identity), acceptance and clarity.

The more the waves came (and there were plenty), the more I could see my self a little better. The more I was fired, the more I could see the entrepreneur within me. The more I was rejected, the more I could see my uniqueness. The self-awareness I needed began to come through the very hardships that, for a while, I just viewed as adversity.

...I hated religion 'cause here was this Christian, he was preaching on Sunday versus how he was living Monday...I was running from Him but He was giving me wisdom...See how the universe works? It takes my pain and helps me find more of myself.

- Jay Z

IX. God Contradiction

Some of the times were so difficult that they forced me on my knees. Growing up in a very religious home and environment, that's all I knew to do - pray. Concerning the undiagnosed illness I dealt with for a long time, it began as simple, frequent stomach pain as a young boy and grew to many symptoms including internal bleeding at its peak in my teenage years. I probably won't forget the times that my body was so racked with pain from the discomfort and dis-ease I experienced that, even as a teen, I would shut myself in a room, get in the fetal position and ask God to let me die where I was. There probably wasn't anyone who really knew I was there

A New Home

mentally. Years and years of doctor and hospital visits filled with uncomfortable tests that required days without eating and inconclusive results left me thinking at times that death was the best and only option for relief.

I don't qualify the pain to have been "from God", but what I believe those moments of questioning and relying on God from a pure place of blind innocence eventually did was push me to see the truth and myself like I never had before. A lack of results, my determination to get them, and life's responding waves eventually reaped the benefits of knowledge and understanding. Before I knew it, those vexatious but timely waves began to take me towards people and through experiences that would challenge my inherited beliefs to show me what was real.

One of the greatest sets of tests that life's waves gave me were the tests of my beliefs. My mind goes back to a day I was sitting in front of a religious leader for an interview to be a pianist/keyboardist and when asked what I was looking for, based upon my past experiences, I started with "I'm just looking for something real". I had been in many situations just like the one I was getting ready to enter and I was tired of seeing contradictions between what I heard being preached by some "men of the cloth" and their reality, and also the reality of all who were listening (to the point of obedience) to what they were saying. It was a system that I was taught was supposed to work. Follow "this" religious rule and get "that" result. Nothing could have been farther from the truth according to the results I saw most people getting. I was tired of seeing some of those same patterns in my immediate family and beyond who were all devoutly religious. I began to see the type of hypocrisy and abuse from a number of leaders that lead me to seek out truth apart from the crowds. The circumstances pulled me away from the irresponsible habit of "blind believing" - trusting those men and women with titles and/or positions and giving them respect as if it was my obligation without any consideration of why they should have my trust or respect at all. I got tired of not seeing what so many said they believed, be their

A New Home

reality. I didn't see, not only what they wanted, but also what I wanted in my life or in theirs. We were almost all bankrupt of real results. If you're wondering what results I was looking for, it's simple: happiness, freedom, peace, love, health, wealth, kindness, fulfillment, etc.; the things that were being posed as possible for me on a weekly/daily basis. But few were living the results and few knew how to get them.

Sitting in some of what I felt were the most religious places on earth let me see some of the craziest, most depressed, mean, unhappy, unfulfilled, broke, hopeless, anxious, fearful, unauthentic, proud people I had ever seen or met. Of course you should expect to see some with those troubles in places where people go to find an answer. The problem for me though was that there were too many people that I witnessed who just turned these meeting grounds into their "drug houses" and never received one. Week after week I often witnessed people get quick fixes that only lasted the length of their rituals and services. It was equivalent to seeing someone be given anesthetics weekly for a surgery that never happens. There was no true change for too many. We'd return home only to live with the same dysfunction we had before going. And here's the kicker: Even the leaders, as a good friend would say, "walked around thinking they were the drug and didn't realize, even they were addicts". Many took on the inauthenticity of those leaders and others, becoming proud, which only further separated them from their ability to get better and to be better. Instead of being honest with themselves and taking on the humility and serious willingness necessary to truly heal and find the results they needed, they would mask their dysfunction attempting to play catch up and fit in with who they determined to be the "spiritual elite". I believe that if they saw behind the masks of some of those same "spiritually elite", some would reconsider their efforts.

These people take pride in their traditions, rituals, titles, and associations, forfeiting the fruit or manifestation of what they say they believe or even actually want. They'd rather appear to have achieved some tainted version of "perfection" than to be who

A New Home

they are and show some level of transparency that could really help someone else or let them know that they aren't alone. These cheap facades avoid the deep-rooted work and responsibility that is needed in order to receive real-faith results. Others in these same environments actually use these tactics to their advantage, pushing their hidden agendas to take advantage of the weak.

Being in large or small isolated groups of people who all have decided to pretend together also avoids any accountability that would require that which is being said to at some point be seen or known. These were not real, result-driven strategies being preached or practiced. Once my eyes opened to it, I couldn't believe it.

Here's what's incredibly and interestingly true about everything I learned from these religious environments and people while there: This describes most of our environments to some degree, whether religious, political, social, business oriented or even family oriented. There are people who wear masks in every environment. There are people everywhere who have and set unrealistic, misconceived standards of perfection that they attempt (and continually fail) to live up to while pretending that they are meeting them. So many of us go to school, work (whether in government offices, fortune 5oo companies, churches and other religious organizations or fast food chains), family gatherings and social events with the intention to fit in, or even worse, to appear to be better than others in that environment, only to return home neglected of the love and results we really need that could come from honesty and transparency. We end up in situations where we're ganging up with those we want to fit in with or those who share similar views as us and often make our group, trivial preferences a matter of right and wrong against anyone who shares a different perspective. It can come out in small topics like "why would they think it's ok to dress that way?" or "this is the way you're suppose to behave on our side of town". And it scales to much bigger issues such as "this is how you're supposed to worship and show dedication to our higher power", or "we have

A New Home

the right angle on how this world should be governed". I have discovered that these strong views and focus on whether your way is right or mine is wrong, always get in the way of what's real with us. We'll never all externally look the same or share all of the same perspectives and that's all right. But the problem with this legalistic type of view where we're calculating our "righteousness" according to our made-up, personal set of rules and standards that make us better than other groups of people is that it always clouds us (with pride) from seeing what's true, what's real and what our personal reality is. You spend so much time trying to be right that you can never get to what's real and what is true in your own life.

I'll give you an example. On a basic level, there a so many of us who calculate our "rightness" or how right we are based upon our desired, "perfect" lifestyle. We feel that if we can climb our way into creating the perfect picture of a lifestyle we've designed in our minds (often pushed on us by outside influences or gained through our misinterpretation of other people's lives), full of parameters and rules and laced with details such as how our spouse and children must look and behave, we'll achieve happiness. We'll determine how much we'll need to make, where we'll need to live, how we'll need to dress, what our weight must be, how long our hair must be and many other factors that would give us the perfect or right lifestyle – all of these being set, not by an internal desire or dream but by an external measuring stick made for comparison.

There are a few things that are problematic with this way of thinking though. The first is that if your standards and rules are what make you, or any other person for that matter, "right", then there's a chance that you may never reach this feeling of righteousness that you so desire. Truthfully, you never will reach that feeling by trying to climb your way to your version of perfection. As a matter of fact, most people throw their ethics and true principles out of the window just to get to their desired destination. It's doing wrong in order to be, or at least appear to be, right. We'll cheat, lie, steal, abuse ourselves and

A New Home

others, if we feel it's necessary, just to achieve this look and mask of an image that we're going for. For many of us, personal worth is tied to accumulation and achievements, and so we'll do anything to get what we're after – to appear to be worth something. This is already contradictory and hypocritical in nature.

Another problem formulated by this ideology is that if it's our standards and rules that make someone right, then when others don't fit our definitions of right, we'll reject, overlook, ignore and oppose them. This is often the cause of sibling rivalry of every kind, from race relations to religion. It has formed consequences ranging from neglect and bullying to mass genocide. Certain non-life-or-death, minor differences and uniqueness's become the very platforms that we judge our "rightness" against. We'll make life-or-death situations out of what could often be respected as a difference in opinion, preference or just an inherent uniqueness.

Thirdly, what this type of outlook does to us individually is block us from our right to have wholeness and real fulfillment in our lives. Let's say that we've checked everything off of our "picture-perfect lifestyle list" (in our eyes) and that the snapshot Facebook, Instagram, and Pinterest (Social Media Platform) version of our lives are "to die for". What any person who has spent any decent amount of time on this earth knows, whether admittedly or not, is that these formulated, calculated versions of perfection don't truly exist within this system of living in which you're trying to be or appear perfect. They'll hardly last long enough for you to snap a picture of it to show. And if you're too busy trying to prove yourself to be right and appear perfect, when those waves I've been mentioning begin to hit your life, as they do for us all, and your "perfect" marriage meets some challenges or your financial security becomes threatened by job loss or some other unforeseen inconvenience, or your children do some things that would embarrass you if it ever gets out; your self-righteous need to prove that your situation is perfect

A New Home

or better than other's will destroy your opportunity to overcome these obstacles by denying you the humility needed to do so. I've heard examples of those who would leave social, support groups when things would go awry in their lives because they'd be too embarrassed to need support!

It's not that it's an impossibility to overcome these obstacles and live on to be a wave runner in every area of your life. It's just that the way to getting these results is not to continually attempt to climb your way to perfection and mask your circumstances to appear to be ok while neglecting yourself the help you really need. Some of us have gotten so caught up in our personas that we begin to believe our own lies. I can't tell you the amount of times I've seen people become ritualistic and programmed to say things like "I believe" or "I'm blessed", or " I'm ballin'", or "I'm a successful [fill in the blank]" or "I'm out here hustlin'", while never really showing any result of what's being said or even being held accountable to it within their circle, if they have one. They learn what they have to say and do to fit in and even will dress the part. After a while, the lack of accountability and results within a group then lead to a lack of consciousness of reality. Pride can begin to form within an individual around the external mask and formalities performed in order to fit in. After this, it can be very difficult to convince someone that saying you are something or dressing the part doesn't mean you actually are it, or that you're being it, especially in isolated environments or cultures.

I've discovered that above our ideologies of what is externally right and wrong, the more weighty issue becomes what's real (true) and what's fake (false).

X. Rebel

I had chosen to be authentic and that meant needing to have authentic results in life. I was not ok with merely pretending I was healthy and whole in every area of my life. I wanted those results to be genuinely experienced for me. I knew my dreams depended on it. I had learned in those religious environments that there are too many of us who just mask our problems or lack of results with God, the same way some of us do it with money, sex partners, addictions, titles, degrees and so on.

Running wouldn't get me results. Hiding amongst the crowd wouldn't fill my holes. Eventually, I got what I needed. But it came in part through being rejected from places I thought I'd surely be received. It came through having the people I thought would affirm and encourage me turn their backs on me only to disappoint and discourage me. But this was the best thing for me.

Bryan Pharr

I remember an instance in particular, in which I was posed with what "my problem" (the reason I didn't fit in a particular work environment) was during what I'll call an "evaluation" from a boss at a job I'd soon be excused from. "It's like…you're too authentic" is what I was told. I couldn't have instantly been more saddened, confused and disappointed by that unexpected hit. I went in to that office with the hope of being able to express, in a greater way, who I was and how I could benefit the workplace I was in and was met with the type of confrontation and unwarranted accusation I couldn't fathom would come of the situation. It was probably one of the most blatant ways that I'd ever been told that who I was being wasn't right for any position I could have held there - as if I was expected to be a made up, different, lesser version of myself in order to survive in that atmosphere. Though the excuse given was a façade for what was really the reason for my being tested and seemingly reprimanded, the fact of the matter was, they were right – not about being too authentic of course. But what was true was that I (my authentic

A New Home

self) did not fit in that position or place. An attack intended to get me off track of my authenticity (and therefore my destiny) was the very thing that birthed a greater understanding of who I was. I may not have completely known who I was but I knew who I wasn't.

Now, for me, the statement "I did not fit" has two implications. One of them is that I really was more than the position I was holding. There were other gifts and "callings" that I would've had to continue to disregard or suppress in order to fit the job. I often stated on that job that I only felt as if I could be two percent of myself. The pain of limiting myself in that way (in hopes of being utilized in a greater way in the future) is unforgettable.

The second implication is regarding my being authentic. I have never wanted to force any situation or relationship period in which I was being tolerated and not celebrated, endured and not enjoyed. Authenticity had always been key to me in business, relationships and in the rest of life, because I needed to know "where I really fit" (where I'd be useful and appreciated) and not where I could force a fit for the meantime, often enduring the pain of doing so, never really being accepted, liked or rewarded for who I am, but rather for a false version of me. I've never really wanted to have to ask "but would they like the real me?" That's all anyone ever gets.

From an entirely different perspective, what I eventually began to understand is that these moments were, sometimes, only mirror images of what was happening with me internally. I was growing into a deeper knowledge of who I was. And these external conflicts were just giving testament to what was going on with me on the inside. Most of the conflicts (born out of the decision to be authentic and centered around not fitting in) were just showing me who I was and the rest were the result of what I was becoming through that growth. It was the result of the waves that were causing my growth and my growth was causing more waves to come. Here's one of the reasons why: People will hardly celebrate the growth you have that they can't take credit for. The ending result of the growth, even if it were just in the area of

A New Home

perspective and realization concerning who I am, would end in me being let go (fired). It would often start with people trying to manipulate my perception of who I was as a means to tame me. They didn't want me to know what I possessed on the inside (gifts/callings) and who I was meant to be. Instances like being fired for made-up reasons such as "not fitting the culture" of a particular place proved not only to show me who I was, but to also confirmed that the uncomfortable feeling I often had in these environments of settling for less than my God-given potential in life was present because…I really was. There was a lot more to me than I went into these situations knowing about. After these things would unfold themselves to me through the many waves that came my way, it would often cause trouble for both me and those who sought to use me for there own plans or control the capacity I'd be used in.

By now, you can probably tell that these "religious environments" were the places I was "let go" from the most. I was mainly a musician professionally for at least fifteen years. Going to places of religious fellowship was the tradition of my family and doubled as the perfect place for me to be groomed as a musician and to get my professional start. What I wasn't aware of, while beginning the profession as an early teen, was that I'd spend so long there relying on that job as a career.

By the time it was necessary to embark on life's journey singly, as a young man, I had already become content with the idea or feeling that I didn't fit in and was perfectly fine with it. That was no problem. The problem was that as life progressed and it was time for me to find a career and job, it became clear to me that I would have to "fit in" somewhere in order to make means to survive – so I thought. This became the ultimate test, because it wasn't like I was just choosing whether I'd try to "fit in" in order to have friends. This was about being able to provide for myself and, essentially, to stay alive. I wasn't graced with rich parents or anyone else who'd have the means or will to just bail me out of any serious financial trouble. This, of course, made me less prone to get in any type of serious financial trouble. But it also meant that,

A New Home

many times, a decision to stay integral to who I was and who I was becoming meant literally not knowing where provision would come from.

For instance, sometimes the mere mention of growing as a person and exploring the "more" I knew myself to be seemed to be grounds for being fired from musician positions I've held. At times I was told that college wasn't even an option unless it left the availability to be a musician on the outside of my schooling, as if my growth and becoming was some extracurricular activity.

Again, because I had already begun my "music career" as a young teen, crossing over into manhood meant making those decisions while I was already operating as a pianist in those environments. Imagine the confusion that can be caused in a young, impressionable mind that was bred to believe that these certain leaders (and bosses in my case) were also the "voice of God" in your life when they begin to try to stifle who you are with their control. Growing and staying true to the dream that was in me literally meant being considered a rebel and fired on multiple occasions from almost every job I've had – every job I've had as a musician.

My identity, in this way, came at a high cost for me. It meant letting go of so much over time. It also meant being willing to die in order to find out what exactly was in me. I had to let go of friends who didn't understand and family who wouldn't accept me due to familiarity. I've had to let go of jobs, positions, people's approval, and so much more. I had so many opportunities to say "You know what? It's not worth it! I'd rather have these friends, that job, this money, this title, that position or their approval than to know what and who I am." I never did. As I became more aware of who I was through these experiences, I had to be willing to evolve, which meant letting the "old me" die continuously. That was just a part of embracing the discoveries I was making and walking in the newfound versions that got me closer to my destiny.

XI. Journey

At other times, it wasn't the waves themselves that showed me my identity. It was what happened within those situations that catered to me. While riding the waves, or at times being tossed by them, I met people who helped me to see me. There were people who began to look to me to be a listening ear and a voice of counsel along the way. It's the very reason I decided to create the brand of and become an "Identity Coach". There were others that were what I believe to be successful business people who I know only took a liking to me because they could see a little of themselves in me.

These big, inconvenient, uncomfortable, and many times, painful waves begin to take me to cities, states, restaurants, businesses, governmental buildings and other places where I continually met people that were slowly giving me bits of insight into who I was. It was the way they looked at me, the way they responded to me, and what they expected of me that began to reflect who I was back to me.

Bryan Pharr

I remember trying to find a job after a big move away from home. It seemed as if the universe itself was opposed to me getting one. I began filling out applications at almost anywhere I could out of desperation. One day, I ended up going into a local McDonalds at a time they were having some type of job fair. There were two lines for applications. One was for a management position, and the other was for every other job. Even having no restaurant experience, I knew I would fair better attempting to become a manager rather than becoming a cook or someone that represented their customer service. It was just an instinct and honesty based from self-awareness. After waiting over an hour to talk to one of their executives who was in town for the day about entering their manager's training program, I was escorted into the office where she was sitting. She was a nice lady who, although she had seen God-knows how many people by now, was kind and listened intently to see whether I'd be a good fit for their program. She eventually asked me a question that I wasn't quite sure how to answer: "How long do you

A New Home

think you'd be a manager here at McDonald's?" I had always been an honest and straightforward person, but I honestly hadn't thought that far ahead. I just wanted to make money as soon as I possibly could. In my mind it was a matter of life and death. I was BROKE! I don't remember exactly what I said, but I'm certain that, because of my desperation to land a job, I wanted to be wise and not lead her to believe that I wouldn't be there for a decent amount of time. I probably made up something that I thought would land me the job.

What I left out of the story thus far was that I accidently showed up to this on-the-spot interview a little unprepared. I normally carried around two resumes. I had already begun to play music professionally and also had already taken a few jobs outside of music here and there. My normal routine was to take my music resume to places that I would apply to be a musician and my odd-job resume everywhere else. I'm pretty sure I printed out the same amount of copies for both but evidently I had been to more restaurants, stores, car lots, gas stations and other places than I had churches or wherever else I applied to be keyboardist. I had completely run out of my "normal" resumes. After finding out that I'd be interviewed by someone that day and needed a resume, I thought fast and figured that I could work around using my music resume to get a management position there. After all, I had run choir rehearsals and taught songs to people who were all older than me at the church my mom attended – some much older than me. That qualifies as managerial experience, right? I used that example and a couple others from the resume to try and convince her to give me the position. She smiled and listened, but through all of my convincing, all of her thoughts began to culminate in that one question; "How long do you think you'd be a manager here at McDonalds"? Next, she began to tell me that she didn't believe that I would be there long at all, and even told me in her own way that she believed that one day, I would become a top influence in music comparing me to a couple of the greats she could think of. I was both

A New Home

astounded and a little disappointed from a short-term perspective.

On one hand, there was nothing on my resume that I believed would even remotely point to, or cause someone to draw a conclusion and prediction as great as hers. I left there having those rare feelings of excitement that I got if I felt or knew someone could actually see me. Whether she was just turning me down nicely, or using her true powers of prediction, that was a moment that I don't take for granted even until this day. She doesn't know that I've gone on to be seen and heard by hundreds of thousands of people if not millions across the world through stages, television and media since then. And I'm still not done with music yet.

On the other hand, I was still physically poor. And just to give you a glimpse of how bad it was; on a separate occasion during my time away from home, I was so depleted financially that before I went to an interview I was scheduled for, I called the lady that was doing it and tried to convince her to give me gas money to come, so that I could make it back to where I was staying after the interview. I had almost completely run out of gas and didn't have any source of income at the time. She said no of course, but after seeing me and probably concluding that I wasn't some sort of con artist, she handed me a twenty on my way out of the door. I made it to that interview on "fumes and a prayer". I still didn't get the job. Imagine that…So I left that McDonalds interview encouraged and still broke. A wave of abject poverty had taken me to a lady who would further reflect back to me, a piece of who I was.

The small, short-lived waves helped me in the area of identity also. These were the times when I would encounter people along my journey and things would quickly go left. I've learned a great deal about who I am and where I fit through the people who have chosen to be my enemies. I've written a lot of quotes over the last six-plus years. You should follow my Facebook, Twitter and Instagram accounts by the way. One of them that I posted on my social networks within the past two years said this: "Sometimes it's

A New Home

your enemy that opens your eyes to your identity". And it's the truth. Again, if you're willing to ride even the small waves, you'll find that they become direction and knowledge to help you. I've been told that I was nothing and a "nobody", and that I should give up my dreams like some of you. I've been kicked while I was down by the people who I thought should be for me as they reveled in my failure secretly. I've been compared to others and measured as less than. I've been considered crazy for thinking I could personally achieve a thing. I've been a victim of peoples jealous and insecure acts within the workplace and outside, just like some of you. But these became the very waves that took me steps closer to realizing just who I was and what I carried. I had to reconsider the magnitude of my own greatness and destiny because of the amount of hate and intimidation that came from people I had no ought with. It made me realize that, before these waves, I had seriously underestimated my own worth, value and impact. I began to see that who I am is much greater than I previously knew myself to be. If it wasn't for theses "small" waves, I wouldn't have recognized or come to terms with my own greatness and potential.

It should be apparent that fitting in just wasn't ultimately ever an option for me. It was never a conscious intent. There were definitely times when I could look back and say that I unconsciously, for a short amount of time, attempted to adjust my authenticity in order to do something that I felt as if I had an obligation to do. But these were often times when my heart was blindly tied to a certain goal or hope, casting an emotional façade over a situation that ultimately wasn't the best for me. I would suffer internally so badly that I would quickly readjust to an up-right authentic position even if that meant letting go of or being let go from the situations themselves. I believe that it's in part due to my decision to never take the measures I eventually saw so many others taking to fit in. It's not something I believed in or ever saw as "worth it". I had made a choice internally to remain authentically true to who I knew myself to be at all times. Truthfully, even early in my life, there was just always something in me that did not like the idea

A New Home

of doing or being the same. I was built differently and was never pressured by my immediate influences, such as my mother, to do so. And to be honest, I don't even know that she would have been able to convince me. I know she would argue the same.

Even today, imitation in the form of thievery is one of my biggest pet peeves or annoyances; but what I had to come to terms with was the cost for authenticity. My journey of acceptance was not only about being ok with the rejection that comes from choosing a different and authentic way or path but also walking out my authenticity with another level of confidence. My pain tolerance for rejection was being built up by the many waves of rejection over the years. After a while, I, the boy who was determined to conceal his difference through silence and avoidance in order to prevent the backlash he knew would come from it, would be willing to become a frontrunner jumping at a chance to be openly authentic and serve a purpose greater than himself. But it didn't come without loads of rejection despite concealing myself. And it didn't come without loads of displeasure and discomfort from trying to contain what was beginning to bubble on the inside of me more and more – my identity, purpose and dreams.

Remember how I said that the universe is bent towards your win? Well I find that particularly relative to my journey of acceptance. Here's the thing, being "authentic" secretly was never going to be enough for me to see my destiny. I had to be willing to be and share my truth, honesty and authenticity openly in order for me to do what I really always wanted to do – manifest my dreams and help others in doing so.

So in come the waves. Wave after wave, all pushing me toward dropping my avoidance techniques and becoming a leader I should have been from the beginning. Early in life, I accepted that I was different but allowed it to push me into a corner and conceal who I knew myself to be at the time. I was genuinely a talkative boy, who loved to dream, draw, make up stories, and make others laugh. Very few got to see that side of me. As I got older, I had to accept that in many cases, trying to conceal myself through

A New Home

what became a lack of confidence or insecurity only proved to make things worse, especially when I had gotten to the age in which it was important to begin to choose how I'd make it in the world. I had already faced many waves of rejection; being overlooked, underestimated, mistook for weak and excluded. I'd even had a couple cases as a teen when I had to verbally and once or twice, physically defend myself in which my opponent quickly found that I was more than what their eyes perceived. But these waves still weren't enough to fully push me out of my cave.

It was when I had to begin to fight for my dreams that made all of the difference. It took me a long time to realize that they weren't just going to happen. I believe that my comfort in quietness came partly from the bad beliefs I carried in which I relied on fate to manifest my dreams. The many waves of rejection had brought about strength and a quiet confidence, but as long as I was waiting on some external force to manifest my dreams, I would continuously be hit with those waves without resolve. I had to learn and accept that and take responsibility

Bryan Pharr

for the direction my life would go in. I had to learn to live out loud regardless of the consequence.

XII. Clarity

I want to share a concept from a post I wrote for my social media presence that I believe encompasses the makeup of a vein to clarity at the core of its message. It was in the form of a video that I entitled "Let Your Past Lead You". As noted before, I don't believe my identity and perspective about my identity would be so crystal clear had I not taken such a deep introspective and retrospective look at life. Here's an excerpt from the video:

"...I don't believe times and events in our lives are their most powerful until we've looked back on them...maybe your way forward is hidden in the bread crumbs of your past...Just like "Hansel and Gretel", we all began our journeys from home. You unknowingly have always left a trail of breadcrumbs (whether in dreams, aspirations, events, moments, realized patterns, interactions, instinctive actions, etc.) that can inform your insight back to the original intent, purpose and gifts in and to you from the beginning. Don't be afraid to let your past lead you."

This was a major key in bringing maximum insight into who I am and who I was meant to be. There are others. But this, for me, tops them all. It brought value to a bunch of events that would otherwise have no meaning. It was the intentional searching for understanding, patterns, value and other "bread crumbs" in general that would ultimately prove to be a catalyst for realizing my identity and purpose. I had to discover them this way because, for me, there were no other options. My interactions with those I admired and looked to (with inner hope) to be a mentor or guidance to me often ended in rejection and dead ends. I never had a personal mentor and was often isolated due to my difference. This life of (near) isolation and a seeming lack of guidance seemed to be the very thing that damned my chances of ever discovering who I was. The waves of life often pushed me into situations with people who, by their control, looked to use others to establish their will or desires in the world. I shared this before: I may not have quite known who I was, but I sure knew who I wasn't, and that alone made me a person who wasn't

A New Home

capable of being under their control for long, if at all. It was as if these waves kept pushing me into predicaments where I was being toughened and tested in this one area: "will you lead or bow?" These conditions caused me to have to find a way outside of someone else's judgment or approval to know who I am.

Now here's an interesting find in my self-discovery process that I would not have noticed had I not been one who was constantly looking for clues to my future through my past: Many of the waves I faced were not just random happenings caused by some outside force. They were the exact result of a young boy who was searching to fill his deep need for affirmation and approval to be who he thought he was. I was raised to need it and didn't know it. I was brought up in a culture that demanded that you be affirmed and approved before you could live out your life's purpose. I grew up thinking something was wrong with me because I wasn't being publicly told who I was or who I could be. I mentioned before that I had a very religious upbringing. It was common to see people having a hand laid on their head publicly by a man or woman of the cloth to affirm them into a role or calling. It was also common in the circles I was brought up in that, at any moment, someone could "prophesy" or give insight into you or a future they said they saw for you if they wanted. I was conscious as a young child that none of these things were happening to me. And probably because I was devoid of affirmation or guidance in the area of identity, it affected me early. I actually believed at one point that I would experience death by the specific age of fourteen, and this was due in part to feelings of being overlooked and not fully cared for concerning my future. It was also the result of how an up-close tragedy affected me at the age of nine.

I've only cried over one death my entire life. By now, I've been to many funerals, especially because, growing up, we went to the funerals of seemingly almost anyone that would die within the church organization my immediate family was a part of. But none of them brought me to tears but one.

A New Home

    I had a cousin to die at the age of fourteen of a head injury on his middle school football field at the end of a game he was playing. We weren't really good friends or anything. And we really only had to see each other because our parents and other relatives associated; or at other times because we had to do things like sit in boring Sunday School Classes and other religious related events together. He was older than me. But his death impacted me like none before or after. I still remember the details of the day it happened. I haven't forgotten how my mom and grandmother got up to rush to the hospital after they heard the news that he had blacked out on the football field. I was left at home with my grandfather due to the nature of the situation. I remember my mother and grandmother pulling back up at our house only a short while after leaving. I was sitting on the arm of our patterned, tan, cloth couch beside the swung open, dark-wood front door; peeping through the black-framed screened door it was coupled with, wondering why in the world they were back so early. They walked slowly from my mother's champagne colored Honda Accord parked on the side of the road up to the burgundy, concrete porch and broke the news to me immediately upon entering the house. "He didn't make it", my mom told me. I was suddenly overwhelmed with a sadness that welled up into tears that I couldn't control. I wasn't expecting to hear that news and was devastated. That death placed a marker in my mind that would make the next five years of my life more complicated to live out.

Somehow his death and a lack of affirmation and identity guidance in my life led to me believing that I would suffer the same fate. I believed that because no one was publically pronouncing to me who I was or what I could do, like I had seen being done for many others (I never considered whether these dealings were even effective, valid or accurate), I was doomed to see death as a teenager. My nine-year-old mind had created a scenario out of an assumed need and a fear. It was the first time I had seen anyone close to me die at that age. And like I mentioned in a previous chapter, things like affirmation weren't common in my home. I watched

A New Home

my mother, grandmother, grandfather and other close relatives succumb to the order of their religious upbringing, culture and system. I watched them and others being told what to do, what they could do, when they could do it and how they should do it – dealing with everything from their gifts/talents to their attire. Simply by being within those systems with them, I was, in a way, being conditioned to rely on someone to do the same for me. Even after I passed the age of fourteen, I was already subconsciously conditioned to believe that my identity had to be revealed or confirmed and approved to me by an outside source.

This formed a pattern in me that became problematic for my self-discovery on many levels. It's the very reason I was such a late bloomer concerning discovering who I was – not that I'm completely done becoming or exploring, but I had very little base or grounding to begin with. It's the very reason I had such difficulty getting along in certain religious organizations and was continually fired. My need for both authentic freedom and affirmation from someone created wars between others and myself almost anywhere I went within these religious constructs. I didn't know that I'd have to give up one over the other in order to have peace. I didn't realize that the boy who grew up fatherless and without guidance concerning his identity was just roaming the world looking for someone who would take him under his wing without selfish intention (to get a job done or to use him) and affirm him into who he was. I was looking for it sometimes in new relationships I'd form and even on jobs I'd take – specifically ones in which the leaders of the organizations considered and portrayed themselves as "fathers", "mothers" and pastors. The asinine thing for me was that many of these leaders would teach that you weren't to operate in or as anything they didn't permit or qualify you to – again, conditioning someone to wait for approval or a co-sign in order to do what they were born to do. But if you were me, someone who was more than what he was being "permitted" or qualified by them to be (a musician), you were stuck without growth and progression if you waited on them. I had seen it too

A New Home

many times – people (some very close to me) who had gifts and purposes outside of their current role or position who either compromised their calling in order to be a part of an organization or fit in; or they'd sit with their gifts and purposes dormant for their entire life waiting to be affirmed or "released". I refused to be one of them.

It all started with a short faze of seeking permission to grow beyond my then current development as a human being within a particular organization I'd eventually be excused from. I then began to explore my growth and potential without permission (on the outside of the position I played within the organization) in quiet hope and expectation that I'd be acknowledged and embraced by leaders I may have respected or felt I may have been similar to. I was always met with intimidation and never long after, accusation and then finally, I'd be fired. After being fired the first time for my unwillingness to be tamed, I went to every other job either looking to establish my own legacy while being a part of their institutions (using it as a means to keep income coming in while I tried to build my vision with my extra time) or again, looking for affirmation to be who I was slowly discovering I was. It was like attempting to join some club of leaders by proving I was one of them. It never worked. I became disheartened when rejected and realized multiple times that the pattern I had previously endured was now in full swing again. I would then soon become distant from others in frustration, sometimes, to try to lessen any further damage to my chances of survival. But like clockwork, my time within these structures would eventually end.

My need for affirmation or validation would continually have me searching for the light at the end of various approval tunnels, and my independent, self-sufficient nature would oppose the very use for the searches I endured. Again, in general, people will hardly celebrate any growth in you that they can't take credit for. I never needed the permission, affirmation and acceptance (normally from just one person) I was searching for, but the lingering, hidden obligations of the teachings of my upbringing had me subconsciously searching. I didn't even realize it. I as

A New Home

well as anyone else who was a similar soul was expected to be and stay a tamed, lesser, suppressed, inauthentic version of themselves in order survive in these environments. These were the waves or events and environments full of control and manipulation that taught me that I'd have to look elsewhere to discover my identity, purpose and overall reason for being here. I realized that I couldn't have both freedom and need affirmation or permission to discover, grow and become. It had to be one or the other.

I wouldn't bow. Fitting in for me in this context would literally have meant giving up my actual authenticity, purpose and fulfillment as so many of you do on a consistent basis. And the cost of fitting in (and ultimately failing at life), for me, was much higher than any cost I could pay by being true to myself and getting excommunicated, rejected, or anything else that could come from not bowing. But this also meant that any clarity concerning who I was would need to come from an internal place. I could no longer look to anyone to help me find me and be me. It was the reliance that I should have been taught and cultivated from the beginning – a reliance on the inside. I had everything I needed to discover who I was, and furthermore, it was always being whispered and shown to me through occurrences, even while I was still searching for someone to externally validate me. This God/internal reliance is the very thing that gave me the skill necessary to do what I've exemplified throughout this entire book…let my past lead me and discover myself, myself. It isn't that I would have to do that now. Once you've switched your reliance completely, you learn to listen all the time – in the present. But I had wasted so much time and ground hoping to find the light at the end of someone else's tunnel through these religious situations and bad beliefs, that at one point (very recently), it became important to make up for lost time. It's part of the reason I'm just now writing this book. Had I known who I was earlier with a certainty, I may have written it years ago. It's not that I had no internal reliance at all. As a matter of fact, because I was raised without my father at home or even a part of

A New Home

my life relationally, I literally looked to God as my dad as a young boy growing up. It was the way I never felt fatherless. This is the very reason I was at war for so long. The strength I had gained from that internal reliance from a young age is what made me authentic and unwilling to bow. But it was my struggle with the culture and systems under which I was raised and involved in that presented these continual tests of whether I'd lead from the inside or bow to the outside.

Once I relinquished myself of the task of searching for the middleman that would release me into my destiny and looked within, I began to see patterns and remember special moments and events that stood out in time to me. I began to remember things like how artsy and imaginative I was as a young boy. I remembered the books I liked to read and the cartoons and movies I liked to watch. I remembered how I loved origami and making paper airplanes from guidebooks I'd buy. I remembered what I dreamed to do when I got older. I began to remember the destiny dreams that I would have at night. I remembered the daydreams I had while driving around Salisbury, NC as a teenager about what I wanted to for people in the future. I remembered how I did on my placement tests at NC A&T...I remembered doing so poorly on my math test that I was put into probably what was the most basic math class available, but scored an eleven out of a possible ten on my writing test. I began to remember when I met God apart from religion and wanted to tell anyone I could about it. I remembered how people would listen to me for hours at a time, talking about it and other subjects. I remembered how many people looked to me for wise counsel without me ever having taken a course on how to give it. I remembered the things I had written and thought nothing about over the years. These and other memories became many of the breadcrumbs that led to the clarity I needed to see who I was always meant to be.

The more I only allowed myself to see myself, the more I could clearly see myself. When I was focused on anyone else at all, whether to fill that void of no affirmation or approval, or even with the

A New Home

slightest bit of comparison for the sake of "me too" discovery (where I'd unconsciously go in the direction someone else was: 1. in admiration of them or 2. out of a need correct what someone was doing by attempting to do it a better way), I'd always fall dramatically short of what I was specifically intended to be or capable of being. I found it imperative to run my own race with the focus solely on it and to, as my mother-in-law would say, "create my own finish line". I've tried to get along with being a part of the crowd I was raised around and more; and the discomfort of having to compromise for someone else's comfort was, for me, unbearable. There is absolutely no feeling comparable to that of being at home in you – no longer searching for a home among the crowds. The feeling of fulfillment in being and becoming only you is like nothing in this world. To walk this journey of life with your soul in tact is the peace that passes all understanding. To boldly live without anyone having a control on your self-confidence and self-esteem, adjusting it by his or her praise or the lack thereof is freedom exemplified. I found clarity concerning who I

Bryan Pharr

was when I cut the middleman that I needed approval from and completely relied on me. What I discovered was the power within to manifest my own destiny from what I hadn't noticed I had the entire time.

Chapter III:

...Fitting in never matters when you're at home within you...

- Bryan Pharr

A New Home

XIII. Where To?

This is the point of it all – the moral to the story – A NEW HOME, IN YOU. The quote I used for this section's heading is the last statement spoken in my four-part visual monologue series entitled "A New Home". It reveals what I've come to realize in my own life and in the life of many others.

Too many of us have gone through life thus far merely attempting to fit in – following all the new trends of our community, living to find our home among the crowd. What we often don't realize is that a need to fit in is the exact thing that prevents us from standing out. You can't have both. It prevents our unique lights from shining. It holds us back from fully seeing ourselves and being able to play the "1 of 1" role we were meant to in this world.

We are the snowflakes of the universe – all of us of the same substance but all branded with our own incomparable qualities. Although we are empowered as a whole when able to live interdependently and within community, our anomalous peculiarities are what bring value to us individually.

To be the same is to lessen the value of the whole. There is and has always been an "I" in TEAM; and to neglect the individuality, personal strength and full difference of the singular puzzle piece is to ruin the picture as a whole. And even if you're someone like me: a person who didn't fit in and was comfortable with that but was trying emphatically not to stand out, you're only doing yourself and everyone

A New Home

else around you a great disservice. You're stopping yourself short of experiencing the fulfillment you were made for and hindering others from benefiting from you as an answer to their life's inadequacies. So where to from here?

I believe that this is the question that hinders so many of us from journeying out and discovering ourselves in the first place. The thought of beginning again from a genuine and authentic foundation, not set from the indoctrination and miseducation of our past from fake people, but from a real knowledge of who we are. "Some of us make our home among the crowds because we can't stand the idea of living with ourselves" (Instagram: @bryanpharr). The truth is that a great deal of us would rather be miserable with company than to endure the isolation and introspection necessary to uncover and bring our true selves to the forefront. It's the thought of beginning again and having to make decisions and take actions (whether small, e.g. posting a picture on the web, or large, e.g. deciding a career path or where to live) that aren't predicated by the approval of parents, peers, friends and other members of our tribes. It's entering into the "scary place" of personal responsibility and leaving the comfort of, in your mind, being able to blame others (and God for some of you) for the unfavorable direction that your life is going in.

Masses of us never leave the car lot of comfort because we can't answer this one question: "Where to"? And the answer has always been to the home on the inside.

The answer has never been to run from crowd to crowd, state to state, community to community, country to country trying to find the place we finally fit. This method of living from the outside in only proves to be detrimental to personal wholeness, fulfillment and happiness. And it always only leads to adjusting one's own authenticity in order to fit into the new place, insuring your disappointment in the end.

This is the cycle of trying to fit in and not having our foundation set in the truth of who we really are. It shouldn't be uncommon knowledge that

A New Home

being a part of a crowd does not fill our voids of emptiness or alleviate us from feeling alone.

My wife would so eloquently describe it this way: "there is a difference between being loved and being understood". When we bend ourselves to fit into certain people groups, we cancel our opportunities of ever being understood due to the fact that we aren't presenting our real selves to be dealt with. This forces us into situations where we can't truly feel loved or accepted, because what we know inwardly is that the love that we may be receiving is for a version of us that isn't real. Thus we feel alone although surrounded by a great many people. Now I don't know that anyone of us would prefer this type of lifestyle over a better alternative, even though it's the norm for most, but there are some of us who have chosen to try to use it to our advantage. These people are those of us who exemplify the epitome of the phrase "selling our souls". Whether on stages, in offices or in homes, there are those of us who have intentionally become inauthentic in order to gain influence, money and admiration. Not only are we forced into isolation among the crowds in this case (continuously avoiding any interaction that might reveal the real us and risk the chance of loosing influence, admiration or stop a flow of income), but in this position, we often become bitter, distrusting and coarse due to only feeling as if people love us for the fame or money we faked/performed to get! These could be described as the wolves of the world who use others only to eventually be used themselves and left destitute when they don't change the course of intentions and actions. Whether choosing an inauthentic lifestyle out of a void or intentionally to acquire fame and "likes"; whether you were taught/raised to do it in your home or whether you adopted it as a means to "get rich quick" and escape financial hardship; whether you formed a new you out of an insecurity because you don't like yourself or a fear that others wont accept the real you; whether you have a chip on your shoulder from old wounds and through you pride are trying to prove to the world that you are somebody; the reasons can seem endless but one thing is sure about it all; if you trade or sell

A New Home

your authenticity (soul) for any external result your fight will always be on the inside and you can never be truly fulfilled.

I've been talking a lot lately (apart from this book) about freedom – about both its benefits and its cost.

Being concerned for the prosperity of your soul and choosing to live authentically is a manifestation of freedom. I don't believe that we hesitate to inter into its glorious riches because we don't always know of its availability, but rather because we are secretly counting the cost and aren't sure if its benefits are achievable FOR US. Sometimes we don't dare to depart from the very little comfort found within the confines of what is often a miserable life because we question our own ability and deservingness of the life we'd truly chase if we looked at ourselves differently. Our asking "where to?"' in this case is our admittance that we believe that certain benefits that life has to offer are only available to an "elite" group of us who are somehow better than we are and have it better off. We think that we were the ones who weren't born with some secret advantage that would make a fulfilled life easy for us; or we mistakenly believe that others were just born fulfilled and merely continued their existence that way into adulthood.

So our response is to settle – to settle in relationships, on jobs, with career paths, in education, in our goals, and really, many times, in every area of life. We decide to just find a fit somewhere. Our dreams then become the very things that eat away at us daily, as our authentic desires to do and be more are continually suppressed. Our crews and tribes that we work so hard to fit into now become support groups that coach us into hating the very dreams that once kept us awake at night. They pacify us and make sure we feel comfortable with never seeing our destiny and potential. Again, we'd eventually rather be miserable with company than to be free and alone. But often, it all starts with a belief that we couldn't make the jump. Even when someone comes along to open our cage (like this book will do for many of you),

A New Home

especially the longer we've settled or remained in captivity; we choose to allow the improper ways we believe about ourselves to override our ability to see the grace and power we've had to manifest our dreams the entire time. Don't let anyone fool you. The cost is the same for everyone. And here's what we don't realize, the cost of a wasted life is much higher than that of a progressive life. It's said that it takes much more effort (and many more muscles) to frown than it does to smile. In the same way, fitting in and being resistant to the authenticity necessary to see your destiny is multiplied times harder than just being and becoming everything you were meant to be. When we don't see ourselves as good enough, strong enough or worthy enough, we begin to try to manipulate the process and find and easier away around to fulfillment or we avoid the process altogether.

There is no elite group. "They" (we) just believe differently about themselves/ourselves. And if no one has ever told you this before, please take it from me. You have EVERYTHING you need to live freely, authentically and to see a good lasting success within you!

I wouldn't be harping on this point so much if I hadn't heard with my own ears some of you literally say "I won't/wouldn't leave this [miserable] situation because I had nowhere to go". Most of you have not even lived with just yourselves long enough to know that God being for you is more than this entire world against you. And trust me, He's for you. If you don't have any one else in your corner, God is! You've lived in such a state of codependence upon your tribes and crowds that you can't see that, again, the entire universe is bent towards your win if you'd just choose to see it. Everything is working for you and not against you.

As for me, I never had the luxury of asking, "where to from here?" as if I had an option to stay. I was fired and kicked out of organizations sometimes so quickly (actually most of the time) and abruptly that even having a plan or a smooth transition into whatever was next for me was never an option. And

A New Home

the incredible thing is that I wouldn't change any of it if I could. I know that, in part, what I had to go through personally is even working on your, the reader's behalf. I can tell you without a shadow of doubt that the fear and insecurity you have about living your truth and God's design and intention for your life that keeps you locked up in the bondage of trying to fit in and settling for less than your fulfillment and destiny, are constructs built upon lies that you've either believed or formed about yourself and the world around you. I've seen the other side. I've been abandoned, betrayed, overlooked, mistreated, not thought (concerned) about, lied to and sold out (lied on). I have paid the cost for freedom and authenticity over and over again. I wouldn't be able to write to you so freely if I hadn't. But here's what I can also tell you – the reward is much greater.

Once I stopped physically running from religious organization to religious organization (after being dismissed from each one), thinking that the next would be different than the last (it took about five occurrences of the same exact results for me to recognize and decide to break the cycle), my only option was to begin again – but this time from a new foundation; a new home. Now let me put this into perspective for you. My entire childhood involved participating in and attending religious events, seemingly non-stop. I got older and began my career as a musician within the same type of atmospheres in my early teens. For the next fourteen years, at least, I would be traveling and playing piano, hoping that I would be able to grow beyond my current position and role into what I always knew I'd be, but while within these systems. I heard stories of individuals going to leaders and saying, "I think I'm called to do ____" and, in many of the stories I heard, the leader gave them support and opportunity to grow. When I attempted it, it never worked for me. When I tried the aforementioned techniques explained at the end of Chapter II in which I took matters into my own hands and decided my growth was my responsibility, it always turned against me. When I tried grounding myself in another career or profession (mainly entrepreneurial pursuits) apart from the establishment I was working for, I was fired. My career life was like trying to maintain a relationship with a girl that just didn't like me.

As a matter of fact, every time we "broke up" it was always in awkward ways. Once, I received a pink slip in the mail and was not contacted by anyone prior to or afterward. Imagine how it was to reach out to the supervisor there about picking up my last check after that one. I've been told I "didn't fit the culture" as my explanation for being terminated. Go figure. Another time I was just told something like, " ...it's time for me to draw the line in the sand...we can't walk together if we can't agree." – no lie! I was the optimistic lover who had false hopes and wanted marriage while she just wanted to use me. I expected too much. I never had any serious offenses or moments of misconduct and was only more frequently accused of being "quiet" and to myself. I guess that scared people. With one job in particular, I made sure to demand that I receive a written statement for why I was being fired. Of course, I never got one. When I seriously reminisce on every individual situation, it really was as if no one really knew what to do with me. And truthfully, that's because I just didn't "fit in". How are you supposed to fire someone for that?

The reason I wanted to give you the width and breath of my situation is so that you know when I say that I had to begin again, I literally meant that I had to begin again. I am at the brink of another birthday as I sit here and complete the task of writing this book. I have spent the last year of my life or more reimagining, failing forward and rebuilding my life from the ground up. I had no footing or solid alternative foundation to start from, except that which was within all along. I didn't have a degree or a well-established substitute career path that I could jump right into, or an endorsement from a single human. And that's not a complaint. The knowledge and experience is well worth the fight. I wouldn't trade it for anything.

But most importantly I want to make it clear that if I can brave these waves, then so can you! This is your master's course on leaving the limitations and

A New Home

inadequacies of "finding your fit" among the crowds – your true self covered and undiscovered, not standing out and being for this world all that you were meant to be. By example, these are the tools and insights needed to live authentically and wholly.

"Where to?" no longer became a question for me to navigate from the outside in, as if someone else had the answer for me. It could also no longer be navigated from the unexpected fortunes of "fate", as if some wonderful life that I knew nothing of was just going to fall on me one day. Discovering me and uncovering me became the simplest process when I began and ended with me. I took everyone and every plan based on someone else's outlook and narrative (or an outlook I had that someone else influenced in any way) out of the picture. I decided what I wanted, where I wanted to be and who I wanted to be. And out of the wellspring of the home that was in me, I remembered and discovered me like never before. So much made sense and I had never been happier with who I found myself to be. When I wasn't trying to see through the partial pictures and perspectives others formed of me with their limited understanding (like trying to look through someone else's eyes to see yourself), my vision became clear. This was in part due to the benefit of isolation. As lonely as it can be, the clarity that can come from it is unmatched in any other predicament.

If we'd let go of the comfort, codependence, and approval of the crowd, we'd discover a life and an us that we never knew existed. If we'd drop the scales of comparison by which we self-sabotage by constantly measuring ourselves against others, we would be free to focus on and discover the genuine strength and the brilliance of our beings individually – the brilliance that was there all along. If we'd be willing to be authentic and find the home within, we could develop a rock-solid self-confidence that cannot be shaken or moved by the opinions of others, swayed by current trends or altered by life's circumstances, good or bad. If we were willing to just be us no matter the cost, we could live a life that is full of fulfillment.

A New Home

"When you build your life from the wellspring of a home within, you no longer look for your place of blessing; you become the place of blessing – You no longer look for the crowd that has what you need; you become an answer – You no longer look to fit in; you live to be a light and to stand out – You no longer live as a cup; you become a pitcher that sources and pours from an endless supply."

"Where to?" – Within.

- Bryan Pharr

XIV. A King And A Pauper

The wonderful thing about living from the inside out, becoming, in time, everything that you are destined to be is that, your worth and esteem are not predicated upon any of your life's circumstances. You've already won at life and you know it. I recently heard an artist describe, in part, what I consider to be the fight for your identity. He stated how we all are at war with ourselves to figure out how to keep dreaming and to discover how we'd inspire both ourselves and others. He went on to say that once we figure this out, life in a way becomes effortless.

I would argue, my friend, that this is the journey of finding "A New Home". It doesn't have to be immediately apparent to anyone around you that you've entered into the wide expanse of who you really are – into this "effortless" life. But in due time they'll all know. The win starts from within. You may only appear as a pauper or servant to most in the beginning. But once you have made a decision and given yourself permission to live the authentic,

A New Home

powerful, significant life you were always meant to live from your unique identity, the king/queen in you begins to rise.

I want to dive a little deeper into the idea that "I may not have known who I was, but I [had a strong conviction] about who I wasn't". I was never very much of a malleable person. It's the quality that has often made me an enemy of the cultures or systems that sought/seek to indoctrinate and ultimately domesticate people. Though there are certain "toxicities" that I've had to deal with and some I am fighting to rid myself of today that have managed to seep through from the environments I've been raised in and exposed to; no system, whether educational, religious, social or political has found me to be a conformist. It's just not the way I was built. I was (and am) the person who was asked things like, "why do you think it's ok to do this [when no one else around you does it]?" or, "what's wrong with you?" if I wasn't attempting to find my fit within a particular group or clique' – a person who isn't afraid to question the societal norms, be myself and, on my own, seek to know truth and gain knowledge. Because this was my nature, coming into adulthood was as difficult, if not more, as you probably have perceived it to be from the picture painted thus far. I was constantly and slowly, through life's many waves, discovering who I was but not quickly enough to go into the many situations I found myself in with a detailed synopsis of my makeup that would properly place me within the organization, if they even needed what I had to offer. Again, I would normally go into these jobs and environments looking to be aided in the task of finding out exactly who I was.

What you begin to learn is that people who are solely focused on getting a job done and keeping a business running can sometimes be more willing to make you into whatever they need you to be rather than to employ you base upon who your were made to be. What these type of employers and managers don't realize is that if they made sure to fill their needs by only hiring people who are gifted or meant for those specific jobs (not that it's their job to help anyone discover their gifts or graces) and invested in ensuring

A New Home

that all employees are operating in areas that are fulfilling to them personally, the success of the company could reach new heights – but that's just an extra tip.

This was the makeup of a cycle for me in which I would, in a way, be so reactive in ensuring that people knew that I wasn't who I was hired to be or who they were making me out to be that my authenticity in this manner would always land me in trouble with the established order. I wouldn't have given up my authenticity regardless, but I wasn't knowledgeable enough to know that I HAD to give up one or the other – either who I knew I was or who they were making me out to be. I would spend days and years within this same career path and position feeling like I was in limbo simply because I would not completely let go of who I was being boxed to be (it was a source of income and a means to an end in my mind) so that I could fully discover and embrace the "more" I knew myself to be. I was being made to make a decision. I was a king being treated as a pauper and I refused to be treated any less than what I eventually accepted myself to be. I may not have known what type of king I was or the type of empire I'd build, but I knew I was a king. And my unwillingness to be molded into anything smaller than the calling that tugged on my inner being daily in discomfort was the very grounds for all of the colorful exit interviews I was privileged to experience.

At one point I was accused of "trying" to be different. Amongst so many people who were making such an effort to "fit the culture" established by executive leadership and founders, I could understand why someone would believe so. This was actually within the conversation that I was labeled as being "too authentic". The truth was that I just wasn't trying to be the same, not that I was attempting to be different. I was myself and it was such a rare sight that it made others uncomfortable and me stick out. I was a king and my AQ (adaptability quotient) had to be the lowest in history. I "deserved" to be fired.

My observation of myself at this point in time, in retrospect, is that as long as I didn't fully realize

A New Home

who I was, I couldn't be comfortable with how others saw me. I'm not endorsing that anyone should allow others to treat him or her with any less respect than any one of us deserves merely because we're human. But what I am saying is that most people are very surface level with their judgments. As much as we're told our entire lives not to "judge a book by its cover", most of us have not graduated from that level of discernment. This means that someone who is absolutely certain of a calling to be a teacher, not only from an internal instinct but from their past experience of being able to effectively communicate and translate information to others in a way they can understand, will only truly be considered a teacher by most when he or she can prove themselves with some documentation of accreditation or maybe footage of a classroom experience.

I was a king and didn't have proof of it. I had enough field experience to know it for myself but not the type of proof that qualified me in the eyes of most. Most didn't genuinely care about a good heart and integrity. They wanted clout and endorsement. Most didn't care about skill and work ethic. They preferred to know what their association with you could do for them. Even if I had the type of proof they needed, I wouldn't reveal it to them. I was concerned with the heart of a person, which is better revealed in their treatment of people they don't believe they need. I was upset with the mistreatment I received in certain places because of the fact that I didn't have the type of proof that they preferred. It reminds me of a girl I started conversing with based from a physical attraction I had for her during my late teenage years. Everything went well until the day we began talking about the future and I decided to share some of my dreams with her. I probably had barely gotten into my multilayered dissertation before she abruptly interrupted with a tone that almost sounded like disgust. "What?!" she asked. "Who are you? You're a nobody! You're nowhere on the totem pole! (She said this verbatim)..." My flabbergasted disbelief almost completely drowned out the rest of her violent barking. After a few of her expressions, I quickly interrupted and, calmly responding, suggested that

A New Home

she makes sure to watch me from a distance so that she is sure to see how much of a nobody I am.

She was no different than some of the rest of us can be. She tried to measure who I was and who I could be by looking at the circumstances surrounding my life at the time. The problem that arises out of these types of situations is that there can be a temptation to prove yourself to those who misjudge you. Now I'm not saying that you can't use these moments in life as fuel and motivation to push yourself into becoming all that you know yourself to be. But it still remains true that what's real doesn't have to be proven. There's a balance here. Essentially, what I'm communicating is that as long as this proving begins and ends with you, prove away. But there is another type of proving that keeps your accusers at power in which you attempt to gain their approval by proving them wrong; or even worse is seeking to stir jealousy or harm someone in proving them wrong. This will always limit your becoming because you will measure your success by how much it takes to get back at someone. And the truth is that your enemy in this scenario will always have power over you. You will only be hurt more when they refuse to give you the approval you so desire or show any signs of care at all while you're striving to affect them emotionally.

I was uncomfortable with the way people saw me, and that gave me something to prove. I saw a king and they saw a pauper. I needed to get to the place where any misconception anyone may have had due to a misguided judgment didn't affect me at all. On one side of the issue I was just tired of literally being disrespected and mistreated by those who willingly abused their authority. But one the flip side, what I didn't realize was that, my need to effectively show and prove to others who I was, was pushing me to discover more than what I thought myself to be. The fieldwork, up until that point, had brought me to certain knowledge, but the waves in my life were continuing to come to carry me to a deeper discovery. What I can obviously see in retrospect is that my discomfort with being perceived by my circumstances and my need to prove to be otherwise was based from

A New Home

a lack of certainty that could only come from making a new home within me. I was still looking forward to a future affirmation. In my own way, without knowing it, I was proving to be approved. I assumed that the more I proved myself, the more I'd be accepted and turned to. I figured that the mistreatment and abuse would stop. In the context of the environments I was in and with the role I played, it only got worse. I needed a "new home" altogether. There was a higher level for me to come to.

It took me deciding to never place myself in the predicaments I had before, but I knew everything had changed once I became comfortable being both the king and the pauper. I became certain of my trajectory and destination through discovery. After breaking the cycles and no longer looking for a "someday", "someone" affirmation, I no longer had anything to prove and could care less if anyone saw a pauper. My kingship was sure and wasn't predicated upon how anyone saw me. And until my rein became obviously apparent to those who judged with misguided eyes, I had become absolutely fine with them defining me by my circumstances. Deciding to make my home within me literally cut my dependence upon the mysterious middleman of my destiny and freed me to be both a king and a pauper. I have nothing to prove.

A New Home

The two most important days in your life are the day you were born and the day you find out why."

- Mark Twain

XV. Alone

I would fall short of my intentions with this book if I only approached the subject of "A New Home" from what you may consider to be a reflective, "heady", principle-based, spiritual, and for some, maybe an almost ethereal perspective. Though this is a normality and niche for me in conversation, I realize it may not be the most effective presentation for all minds, especially when not partnered with a more tangible expression. Let's talk about the practical nature of finding "a new home".

Now I have to warn you. This is the part of any transfer of information that makes all the difference. If principle never turns to practice, regurgitated information alone will prove to be ineffective for life transformation. The difference between what's real and what's fake in this world is often categorized simply between what's lived and what's only learned.

I have done due diligence to ensure that everything presented in this narrative is actual knowledge gained from my life experience.

I should also warn you that it's the fear of turning what's learned into what's lived that hinders most people from seeing the fulfillment in life they deserve. But what's important to remember is that, in cases like this, you're hearing the testimony of someone who has already passed through what he or she is inviting you to pass through, through the information provided. This means that if he, she or I could make it, then so can you. There has to be something wonderful on the other side if anyone is willing to ensure safe passage through written example. This doesn't mean that it won't be scary or that it'll be easy but it does mean that it'll be worth it. There is no benefit to what you take in if you don't work it out.

A New Home

Finding "a new home" is about deciding to take up residence within and discovering who it is you really are. There is a quote I wrote that I recite often. It states, "Fulfillment doesn't come from changing into things you aren't but rather by becoming everything that you are". The two truths that are vital to draw from this statement are that: 1. You were created with intentionality and with a purpose. And: 2. Personal "life" and fulfillment are going to come from becoming and manifesting everything that you were intended to be. The hard thing about discovering what and who you are (or what your were intended to be) is escaping the distractions that are surrounding us at all times long enough to do so.

From the time we are born, there are judgments being made about us and plans being made for us. From our parents to our education providers, our government officials to business owners, we are being pitched to and pushed in a number of directions from the get-go.

Bryan Pharr

It starts with our parents examining us from the very beginning. If we're "long" or seem to be tall babies, we're often declared to be something like basketball players. If we're stout we may hear things like "that's my little running back!" If we are considered smart in our adolescence, we're probably told that we would make good a good lawyer or doctor. The list can go on and on. Sometimes what's being pronounced over us is nothing but a parent's or close relative's selfish dream for us.

That's not even to mention the aptitude, personality and other "potential" measuring tests that score and categorize us in school. We can be swayed by the results of these types of tests from the time we enter schooling at a very young age, all the way into the early stages of our adulthood and beyond.

On top of that, we have cultural and other influences gained through media intake; or even organic influences gained throughout life such as the teacher, aunty, uncle, boss, or person in the

A New Home

neighborhood that just really took to us and decided to take us under their wing.

We also have to consider booms in industries and changes in the economy and world climate that often influence and affect our viewpoints on our identities. A rise in entrepreneurship, for instance, seems to make a lot of people who never considered that lifestyle all of a sudden identify with it in an effort to keep up.

And we still haven't acknowledged influences like where we were born, who we were born to, the conditions we were born into, our ancestry, the belief systems and traditions we come from that are passed down to us, and even relational influences that come into play when we do things like "fall in love" for the first time.

All of these influences and more can serve either to hurt or help our chances of discovering who we are – either as direction or distraction. From my experience, unless highly focused and well picked out, more can be harmful and distracting than helpful.

Bryan Pharr

...Which brings me to my first point of practicality, and that is to discover yourself, by yourself. Now to be clear, what I am not saying is that no one and nothing can help you discover your identity and purpose. The portions of my story that you've read thus far alone would discredit that statement if that were what I meant. Even what you wish would never happen to you can be more of an agent to further your knowledge than sometimes what we wish would happen. What I AM saying is that your discovery should begin and end with you. Your instincts, intuition and ability to reason are all there to help guide you through your life's journey. You need to trust what's in you above all else. You'll need to take personal responsibility for who you're becoming and where you're going. Starting from "home" or from within then places a filter on any input, whether information or experiences, that can sort out how you see what's being presented and whether what's being presented should be considered as either "food or waste".

A New Home

The reason this is important is because, even with the best intentions, not everyone's assessment of you and of life is accurate. And truthfully, no matter who you're talking to, we are only able to contribute information from what we've learned, what we've experienced and what we believe. So in the case that you're talking to someone who is misinformed, hasn't left the twenty mile radius of their city their entire life, and has bad beliefs; you can weigh and measure any direction they may try to give you with something other than a, "that's not what my mama said" type of reasoning. Your mom might be the one with the bad beliefs.

What I am ultimately suggesting is that you "kill the middleman". The middleman in this context is any point of codependence that allows, permits or causes you to live irresponsibly and without intention. This can be a parent, a priest (preacher, rabbi, spiritual advisor, etc.), a boss, a group or clique, a spouse (boyfriend girlfriend, etc.), the government, or even a "god"...You'd be surprised at the amount of people who are blaming God, who is normally their preacher in disguise, for their lack of fulfillment and purpose. But again, that's for an entirely different book. You have to take control of your life. And that means taking it from the places we so easily have given it over to without question. These points of codependence are the influences that are able to inform you, make judgments about you, mold you and impart to you without question or reasoning. You are ultimately responsible for the outcome of your life and to give up that responsibility in any direction is a sure way to never see the full extent of what you were meant to be.

Establishing "a new home" is about taking your power back by betting on you at the end of the day. You're going to have to stop being lazy and just allowing people to tell you who you are and what to believe and letting them place parameters on how much you can be and have. You're going to have to do your own research and make time to isolate yourself so that you can get to know yourself. You're going to have to learn to love yourself, appreciate yourself, forgive yourself, reward yourself, encourage yourself,

A New Home

invest in yourself, be confident in yourself and even permit and affirm yourself. This is the essence of establishing "a new home" within.

Now what I have to warn you about that's on the other side of taking full responsibility for your own life is that, this is the quickest way to expose the wolves and snakes in your life – the ones that have been preying on your codependent nature. If you are a person who has been easy to control or has given up control easily, you may have an entire ecosystem of controlling, manipulative people around you. Your deciding to take your power back may initially cause you to loose everything. Controlling, codependent people love codependence and will possibly respond ferociously when they feel they have lost it in an attempt to regain it. But don't let anyone fool you. They aren't your key to fulfillment. You are. He or she isn't the gatekeeper for some blessing you're waiting for them to bestow on you someday or that's just going to fall out of the sky because of them. Your blessing can be found on the inside. You aren't incapable of taking care of yourself and creating for yourself the life you've always dreamed of. I don't care what your level of education is, how long you've gone without establishing yourself, how deep you've dug a hole for yourself with your actions and behavior, where you're from or what your current circumstances are. You have everything you need to be a hero in your own way to your generation and to this world.

But you're going to have to be willing to discover who you are and what your purpose is for being here. And that's going to stem from your willingness to be alone – to live with yourself long enough to find out. You're going to have to drop your codependence, no matter the relationship(s), and possibly lose the relationship(s) because of it. It might be parents, a spouse or even a job. It may be all three and more. You have to start with you and build a foundation from your willingness to be at home in you first. You have to burn your need to fit in. You have to rely on and trust in you. You have to be ok with standing out. You're going to have to be willing to endure hardship (i.e. physical, mental, financial,

A New Home

etc.) and persecution (being talked about, misunderstood and possibly mistreated). You have to be willing to put in the hard work and figure life out, even if you have to do it alone. This also means you'll have to develop the ability to self-motivate and to develop self-discipline. You're going to have to be authentic and stay true. The more favorable predicament would be that you don't have to do it absolutely alone. But you need to be willing to, just in case. Either way, even with one or two to walk with you through the journey, it's still extremely lonely simply because of the inward work you have to do.

Here's what you need to understand. Going through life inauthentically trying to fit in all of the time does not make you "not alone". I would argue that that lifestyle is even lonelier for a number of reasons. One of them being that you can never gain true friendship with someone that you're faking with in order to be friends. This is because the ground of your entire relationship is built with shifting sand. It adjusts according to whomever you're talking to.

Another is that, not only are you lonely in the crowd but, because you've traded your authenticity for company, you can't even be at home with yourself apart from the crowd. You don't even know who you are.

Furthermore, that lifestyle is not preventing you from being misunderstood, mistreated, talked about or used. It's actually more likely. It is not preventing you from hardship. Your safety is an illusion. The worse thing is to be lonely and surrounded. The worse thing is to be mistreated, used and going through hardship without anyone in your corner that you can genuinely call a friend.

I'd rather be alone, be at peace and at home within myself than to never love myself. I'd rather know who I am than to get so lost in the many versions of myself I created to gain and keep the crowd, that I can no longer tell which parts are real, if any. I'd rather be alone and be fulfilled than to be a leaking bucket of "success". I'd much rather have one or two genuine friends and sometimes feel lonely than

A New Home

to be surrounded, be absolutely destitute of true friendship and literally be alone. I'd rather endure hardship that comes as a result of my decision to be authentic and to stay true to who I am than to endure hardship as a direct consequence of my inauthentic, shifty dealings. The list is extensive but I hope that my point is coming across clearly.

The choice isn't really whether there is a cost to pay. You'll pay either way. But there is only one way that really results in reward. With the other, even what seem to be the rewards (i.e. getting to take photos with the crowd, "job security", getting to appear successful, etc.) are all unfulfilling and fleeting. You're trading your soul for the appearance of success and happiness. The choice is really whether you want something real or whether you'd settle for a lifetime of stressful faking and maintaining to one day regret not ever seeing what life could truly be had you went all in on you.

XVI. Different

My second point of practicality involves doing something most people who have made their home among the crowds would almost never do – try something different. This may sound absurd and you may be thinking, "What? People I know try new things all of the time…doesn't everybody?" But let's take a deep dive into the issue. Firstly, the answer to the question "doesn't everybody?" is an absolute no. And secondly, in this context, I'm not just talking about trying new things in general. What I mean is that few people try things apart from the trends and the approval of their "tribe" or group. So many of us have inward desires to do more and be more. But in order to accomplish these things, we'd have to try or "taste" things that would normally not be an option for those surrounding us. This could be anything, ranging from something as small as changing your hair color to a shade considered outlandish within your circle, or to something as large as deciding to choose your own spouse when you come from a culture of arranged marriages. I'm talking about making the decisions that may have a price tag attached to them – breaking the norm of your clique or gang. Some of you already know you're different but just aren't outwardly, actively being it. If you want different results than what you see around you, then you HAVE to do and be differently than what you see. For example, if no one is happy or successful around you and you want to be happy and successful, then you have to break out of the dysfunctional patterns those people have and form new ones that will lead you to that goal. This means that you will have to, again, start with you, try different things that may not be approved by those around you and keep trying things until you learn how to get where it is you're trying to be. One of the ways that you'll discover who you are, is to be willing to try as many things as you need to until you build a certainty of your identity within you.

Let me shed light on a thread of my story that I have not yet fully exposed here. Concerning my interests, I've tried just about everything. I've always been someone who loves to create and my instincts were great concerning that matter. Even at a very young age, it would be the very thing that kept me in trouble in school. I have had to turn a number of cartoon drawings over to my teachers for allowing their instruction time to be when I decided to brush up on my character art. It turned into "a thing" and a few people even asked me to draw something for them; or asked for a drawing I had already done so that they could paste it on the front of their notebooks to set them apart from everyone else's. Later, my mom's instincts and insight were good in that she decided to invest in me in the area of music. From learning to play the saxophone she bought me for middle school band, to learning the synthesizer/sequencer I just had to have as an early teen that would reveal and confirm my passion for music creation, my knack for music became obvious.

I would go on test more of my interests in the realm of "higher education". I've been saying five but I'm just now realizing that I am a SIX-TIME college dropout. (One thing's for sure; I don't give up on

A New Home

myself easily) I went to school for business three times. I went for psychology twice. And at the last school, I rediscovered my love for art, but in digital form. I went to the Art Institute of PA Online and ended up dropping out after receiving my majorly discounted, professional design software and realizing, as always, that the classes, for me, were incredibly hard to endure. I was moving along quickly in learning how to use the design software provided while my classes were covering things like the "art of 1685". This reignited passion turned into entrepreneurial pursuits such as designing and selling a custom t-shirt line and branding other ventures I'd pursue. My love for music creation would turn into creating a plethora of songs and at least three albums with my family and more. It would also aid on the many jobs I've taken as a musician.

I've also been a janitor and have taken a couple hard-labor jobs on the side and seasonally (They weren't interests. I just got them for the money.).

I tried relocating to see if that would help in my journey any…I tried creating a forum through which I would teach classes about God and faith…I am currently in the start up phase of a business geared towards the "becoming" of all people…

There's more, but I'm certain you get my point. What I also need to point out is that I wasn't following anyone's blueprint. The circles that I grew up around have generally been VERY much more conservative and patterned. But I've never wanted their results. I had to try something different.

My most recent venture that I decided to end is one that I really want to highlight for a couple of reasons. After being shunned from the religious world multiple times for my difference and deciding never to put myself in that position again, my wife and I chose to rebrand the last company I mentioned above and make it a "church". Now, the reasons we did this were that, over the years, we had become somewhat of mentors to some of the people we met within these religious realms and because it was the language of

A New Home

their culture, they began to call us pastors. I also come from a line of pastors – my father being one of them. We also wanted to do something about the mistreatment, corruption and what we felt was a lack of substance that we saw on a regular basis within that community...so in a way, it seemed sensible. Our idea was to completely disrupt that world and design a completely new system that we thought would better serve the people from the ground up. Our idea was great because it came from a great place, but overall, it just didn't make sense to do. So, for a number of reasons, including that we didn't want to be represented that way as people in the world, we decided to dissolve our venture after just two months in and publically renounce any association between what we're doing and that world ("church").

I wanted to highlight this story firstly because I don't know anyone personally (well, maybe one or two) that would have done what we did. I told my wife how proud of us I was shortly after we made the announcement. We had made another announcement just two months before declaring what we were going to do without anyone's permission, assistance or endorsement. What makes the situation so unique is that it's not the way of thought in that world or many worlds. The thought is that EVERYONE has to be affirmed, approved, licensed, endorsed, etc. to even consider beginning a work like that. The fact that we were even using some of the language from that world to describe what we were doing was causing some to be stirred. People wanted to know who was going to be "watching over" us, who had approved of us doing so, and so on. It was kind-of insane.

But this certainly describes many of our situations. Being surrounded by people who need permission and need to be cosigned or publically affirmed will always lead to you and your freedom being questioned if you are a person who walks and grows freely. They won't understand if you make a decision that reaches outside of the limitations and parameters established within the rules of their group.

What I was proud of the most was not that we made that type of decision. That was normal for me.

A New Home

Again, it's the reason I didn't fit in the first place. What I was proud of is that we were able to be both the king/queen and the pauper – We had nothing to prove. How many of us would have done the same? Some of us are so busy proving ourselves to others that we got ourselves into situations a long time ago that we should have ended. But we keep up the charades for fear of embarrassment and a fear that our pseudo masks of perfection be removed revealing the real us. This again, is the outcome of forming a home within you – not needing the praise or approval of men and not having anything to prove. This is how you gain the ability to keep trying things and keep trying things (if you need to) in order to really dial down on who it is you are and what you're here to do. I've always used my instincts, my intuition and listened to life but still have had to try a great number of things to grow to the certainty I have today. I am more confident of my future and my success than I have ever been simply because I put in the work to discover my identity. I questioned, researched and above all else, tried different things that most people around me weren't willing to do. It will be the same for you should you decide to discover who you are. You have to be willing to defy the laws and the expectations of your group and do what sometimes will be scary to try. You'll have to be willing to push your limits and be uncomfortable. But again, this means that your actions cannot be predicated upon the crowd. You'll have to have a sure foundation so that the winds of trends don't blow away what you're building on and adjust your identity with every new wave of ideas from the outside.

Be different so that you can be you. Being authentic includes embracing your difference and being comfortable with living it out. We need more of it in our world today.

XVII. Icon

This brings me to my third and final point of practicality - and that is to STAND OUT.

One of my favorite songs introduced to me through one of my favorite childhood Disney movies, "A Goofy Movie", is "Stand Out" performed by Tevin Campbell. That song still rings in my head every now and then till this day. It exemplifies the attitude of someone who has decided to be at home in themself.

The thing about discovering who you are and why you're here is that, at that point, you can become an answer. Everyone's purpose involves becoming an answer to the world around him or her in some way, shape or form. Whether through making them laugh, informing them, inspiring them, taking care of them, healing them, leading them, giving them creative escapes and a multitude of other things, when you become an answer or the cure to a problem in the world surrounding you, you want nothing more than to administer it to as many people as possible. You go from fitting in to literally doing whatever it takes to stand out as a beacon of light, letting everyone know you're someone who possibly has something they need.

Let me take a quick turn and be honest with you about something here. All of the times I was rejected didn't hurt me because I wanted to fit in so badly. I have been a loner for as long as I can remember. It hurt me because I knew I was an answer. And I wanted so badly to be one for the people I was being rejected by. Even my proving for affirmation in the past was just so that I show that I was an answer. It's even why we more recently decided for a brief amount of time to do the whole relabeling deal with our business – to hopefully find another way. But each time I was slightly shortcutting my own process. I now realize that you can't lead and want to fit in.

What I'm saying is that, if you aren't carful, desiring strongly to be an answer in the lives of people you love and want to help can result in you

A New Home

bending and suppressing your authenticity for their comfort also. I had to become comfortable with, and I am still becoming ok with the fact that I can't be an answer for everyone. In fact, me attempting to be an answer in the lives of many in the circumstances I found myself in actually only turned out to be me trying to make people go places they never wanted to. I would listen to the complaints of some who would be within the same circumstances, empathize with them and determine that I would want to be an answer for them in some way. I would do this only to later find out that many times, they were only complaining and didn't want change or "help" at all. They wanted to change everyone else. I went to great lengths to extend a hand and bring people where I was and get them to come where I wanted to go – even adjusting minor portions of myself as to present something they would not be afraid or uncomfortable to follow. In the end, I only found it to be counterproductive in the effort to become an answer at all. I needed to see that I had to become more and more of an answer for myself before being able to do that for anyone else – and even then, you can't take everyone with you.

Truthfully, the rejection I was receiving was all the affirmation I needed – to let me know that I was attacking this very issue, "being an answer", from the wrong level. I could not help the crowd disguised as one of them. This was an old inward dilemma showing up in new situations. I knew I was a king and an answer, but still hadn't quite figured out that you can't avoid boldly standing out and stand out or be an answer simultaneously. I couldn't see that if I was in a place where I had to "fly below the radar" in order to avoid controversy or in a place that I had to suppress my authenticity in order to be appreciated and not just tolerated, I could not lead or be an answer on that level, or with those people. But the crowd was sure to let me know in its own way at every stop I made on life's journey. "You're not one of us!" You're opinionated!" "You're too authentic"…etc. They would always "spit me out", letting me know that I was flying too low or in the wrong place.

A New Home

If I could paint a picture and use it as an example, it would be represented by a CEO (someone who is an owner and could naturally solve problems on that level) taking a job as janitor and attempting to solve problems within an organization at the level he was gifted to but from the position he had decided to work from. Now in a movie-like scenario, which is what I believe I was always secretly hoping for, someone high-up in the organizational chart sees the janitor for who he really is and gives him a job that more suits his natural abilities. Wouldn't that be the ideal outcome? But sometimes the janitor is considered as a threat and is dealt with in a way that more resembles attempted murder than promotion.

I believe I have detailed my past plenty concerning this matter by now, but here's the new point I'm trying to make this go-round: Standing out meant that I could not continue to take the outward position of a janitor over and over while inwardly being the "CEO" I eventually, through numerous cases of rejection, uncanny affirmation and uncomfortable settling, came to fully accept I was. It didn't even make sense. I was running from the level of impact and leadership I was meant to hold. No matter if those in high positions dealt with me from the viewpoint of a friend or foe, whether kindly or harshly, the truth remained that I could not effectively lead the way I was geared and graced to from the way I was allowing myself to be positioned.

"Why don't you go do your own thing?" It's what I was actually asked by a CEO while working within his organization. And though intended to be harmful, it was questions like these that kept me cognizant that I could not be permissibly ushered into the full measure of my being. I had to take full responsibility for that outcome, fully trusting that I had everything it takes to get there and be there, killing off the expectation of a middleman relation.

The teachings of my past informed me improperly and for a while, kept me in cycles of not thinking enough of myself, and flying way too low. The fact is, sometimes we can have promotion in

A New Home

mind when what was always in mind for us is platform...but that isn't for everyone.

I had to continue to be willing to do what the crowd wouldn't dare to do and be what the crowd wasn't willing to be – but apart from the crowd. There had to be a clear distinction and acknowledgement between who I was and who the rest of the world was in relation to me. Of course discovering that distinction was the process of being authentic and trying different things somewhat among the crowd for me, at first. It wasn't until the continuous reminders that I didn't fit the status quo of the groups that surrounded me pushed me to find a new home that I began to take standing out to another level; and being informed through my circumstances, began to dream differently.

Practically, the process, at a certain point, became more fully becoming "an open book" and finding new ways to publically translate and communicate knowledge and truth. I did so in ways that naturally presented themselves to me and in ways that I felt I was gifted to communicate through. These included written, verbal and artistic methods. I began to use social media platforms to produce content that utilized these artistic measures. I began working on small film projects for the web and even hosted live events.

This was a far cry from the behavior of the young boy some people thought was a mute. I was willing to do what it took to stand out even when it created uncomfortable circumstances for myself; because, avoiding the calling in order to fit in presented the greatest agony.

Even with that being true, the discomfort of displaying my truth for the world to see was significantly tough to endure, especially in the beginning. This is what I meant by saying "the process became becoming an open book" – putting my truth on display.

If I could tell you the amount of times I had written a personal post for a social media page and felt so much anxiety about it that it would literally

A New Home

take "too long" to post (after about a hundred edits) and then put my phone facedown or hide it due to feeling anxious about the response, you wouldn't believe it. Even now, writing this book presented moments where I was almost brought to tears, reminded of pain I'd like to forget and even for a couple moments, was embarrassed about what I was willingly pushing myself to share. This type of thing isn't for those who are easily offended and softhearted. My sheer desire – this inward obligation, overrides every opposing feeling every time.

How does this apply to you? Well, whatever your method is, whatever you were created to do, be sure you stand out and do it. The point of leaving the way of "the crowd" and finding "A New Home" within you is so that you can, again, discover your personal identity, live authentically and to also in turn, become an answer.

This was never about going off into seclusion and "becoming your own God", isolated from the rest of the world. It's so that you can become an answer for those who need you and those you CAN help, which won't be everyone. This is what is ultimately going to bring fulfillment to your life. Once you learn to lead a life of fulfillment from the inside out, the point is to show other individuals within the crowd how to lead their own lives. It's a full circle movement. This is what leads to "life more abundant". This is the key to your significance. It's the pattern and access to your wealth, health and a new level of wholeness. To go through life just blending in with the crowd, living with little intention or responsibility, being dragged by life; never learning to ride its waves only to look up and try to make sense of things before you die, would be a complete mismanagement of the enormous potential latent within every fiber of your being.

    I learned something major along this journey thus far concerning standing out. I wasn't thinking big enough – personally or in general. As long as I was only willing to stand out among the crowd, bending to make them comfortable and being unwilling to accept that I may never be able to help

A New Home

some I loved, which never worked out for me anyway; I could only hope to be an influence to a few. But one thing is certain of everyone I admire today and throughout history that are considered cultural icons. They never made their home among the crowds. I had to learn to let go of the things that would only allow me to be an influence and embrace what it takes to become the icon I'm willing and on a path to be. It's, in part, the choice to comply with your dreams and to stand out.

You don't have to ever leave the crowd to be an influence; but the centeredness it takes to walk your own path, whether with a few or alone, whether considered brave or foolish by others – to become an icon can only be the result of your decision to make your home within you and authentically stand out no matter the cost. You cannot be defined or legislated by the opinions of the crowd or even affected by their determining of you. Why just settle for an influence when there's the choice be an icon? Why fit in when you can stand out?

XVIII. Legacy

My final wish for you within these written pages is to be in it for the long run. There's a price to pay whether you decide to fit in, compete, live inauthentically and be governed by the crowd, only to regret what you've built and are becoming; or whether you make a new home within, stand out, be free, be persecuted for it, feel lonely (although never alone), be at peace in your soul and learn to lead a life of fulfillment.

The price for both is the same – death. One, you live to die. The other, you die to live. Especially when considering the pseudo success that can come from fitting in, you may think there are some benefits to both. Maybe we should approach the decision from a different perspective – longevity.

First we need to ask ourselves, "How long can this last?" The problem with is fitting in is how much you have to do in order to do so. Everything from your dress (attire) to your personality, to your

A New Home

mannerisms to your career choices, to your esteem, to your pay, to your parenting, to your beliefs, to your activities, to your associations and on and on, are fair ground for the crowd to dictate. This puts you in the position of having to "maintain your membership" and most likely keep up with a set of qualifications and rules that you may have never even considered if you lived freely. People will often lie, become manipulative, competitive, conniving and even "murderous" if anything or anyone threatens their "group membership". People will also do the same to join. You're constantly playing "keep up" and aren't being fulfilled by anything. You have to constantly wear a mask so as to not let anyone know what you really feel and to maintain an image of "perfection". What you have to eventually come to ask yourself is, "How long can I keep up the antics?" "How long can I keep jumping through hoops for people who aren't really concerned about me?" "How long can a relationship or system built upon lies really last?" "If it only takes the truth to desolate it, how long before someone breaks and decides to be honest?" "How long can I keep up this performance?" And for some, "How long can I keep track of all the lies?"

Living authentically takes the "effort" out of living. There's no one to perform for and nothing to prove. There are no lies or masks to keep up with and no memberships to maintain because you are no longer living life from the ambition of "finding your fit" or fitting in. To the contrary, and I haven't mentioned this yet; your fit will begin to find you. You don't start relationships and find out ten or twenty years later that you never knew the person you were with. You no longer adjust you persona to get what you want. You take control and are no longer bound by the rules of the group. This allows for the freedom and ability to expressively find you and be you. Your inner peace will be, in part, due to your decision not to trade or sell your identity (who you really are) for riches, fame, attention and the like. You won't have to hide to keep from showing the real you at times when you aren't performing. You'll be yourself at all points. Any success gained will not be in danger of being snatched away should others see the real you. The

A New Home

crowd will no longer dictate or control your success. Your ability to experience "life" and success will become effortless. I don't mean without work, but rather that the "work" itself will become pleasure.

The final question we need to ask ourselves is, "How long will this last?" Although this and the first question may seem similar and may be considered the same to some of you, the context is completely different. This time we're asking how long what we've accumulated while walking either path will last. What will your legacy be? Will what you've built crumble before anything can be passed down due to the facades and lies you've built it upon giving way under the pressures of real life? Will you have built anything at all, being distracted by trying to fit in and making sure you don't leave the safety and the comfort of the crowd? How will those who come after you (specifically your offspring and their offspring and their offspring) view you. Will they even know you? Will they feel as if they are starting from or coming from nothing and as if you left them without the slightest bit of a roadmap, accountability or aid? Or will you be brave enough to meet the man/woman in the mirror and make your home in you so that you can find and fulfill everything that was there from the beginning?

The destiny that was designed for every one of us has always been great and has always led to our significance. We as people will not become everything we were meant to and see that destiny while measuring ourselves and making our home among the crowd. That codependent, copy and paste process may seem to be a quick and easy way to get the things we want but "quick and easy" in this sense, won't last. It's the process of becoming authentically that forges the fortitude, character and strength it takes to build something that will ultimately be long lasting. Only thinking of what we want now in order to maintain our crowd status, keep up and compete, will leave us lost and without a legacy. It's a sure way to be dragged around by trends and waves so much so, that all we will leave is a trail of confusion marked by unfinished business. This is the fate of those of us who want to fit for now.

A New Home

It is my desire that you consider life in the long run – that you consider your children and their children and so on. It is my desire that they tell of your story, and long after you're gone, remember the quality of life you lived and made available for them. It is my desire that it be told both far and wide. This is the fate of the one who was in it for the long run, and for those of you who decide to find "a new home".

#ANEWHOME

Bryan Pharr

It's Written

"As for my legacy, it is sure. I've made a decision to "die to myself" and find "A New Home" - within. My legacy will spread both far and wide. I will continue to be and build a platform for truth and be a bridge to freedom. I will help countless of you find a new home. This is just the beginning."

- Bryan Pharr

ABOUT BRYAN PHARR

Bryan Pharr is a writer, producer, inspirational speaker, and coach who is an emerging, leading voice to his generation and beyond, preparing and equipping them for an abundant life. His message is clear. He desires that all people would come into a full knowledge of who they really are and lead lives that are full of fulfillment. As the founder of IEXIST (becomingallthatweare.com), a coaching and counsel company geared toward the betterment of all people, Bryan is constantly working out effective ways and strategies to inform and inspire those who need it, in an effort to push them to become all that they are.

LET'S STAY CONNECTED:

Facebook: facebook.com/bryanpharr

Instagram: @bryanpharr

Twitter: @bryanpharr

Bryan Pharr

www.ingramcontent.com/pod-product-compliance
Lightning Source LLC
Chambersburg PA
CBHW030111170426
43198CB00009B/578